Dining
among the
Stars

A celestial compendium
of creative cuisine
by leading performers and artists
from around the world.

Compiled and edited by

MICHAEL PAUL CURRY

*Stephen, maestro —
lirily fratestrements, much love
and affection! respect
as ever
Michael
May 2016.*

PUBLISHED BY

124 Byrd Court, Clarendon Hills, Illinois 60514

www.mpcarts.com

DESIGNED BY

Phoebus, Virginia • www.mellenst.com

COPY EDITORS

Judith Laura Romans & Eileen Meindl O'Hagan

PRINTED IN THE UNITED STATES OF AMERICA

Signature Book Printing, Gaithersburg, Maryland

Proceeds from the sale of this book are being donated to Drepung Loseling Monastery in Atlanta, in helping to foster compassion and to facilitate His Holiness the Dalai Lama's vision for the convergence of science and Buddhism for their mutual enrichment.

www.drepung.org

Geshe Lobsang Tenzin Negi (center) with His Eminence Cho-Sang Rinpoche and the author.
Photo: Liz Greene

Foreword

It is with great pleasure that I accepted Lama Michael's kind invitation to write the foreword to this delightful book, *Dining among the Stars*. While I do not profess to be an expert on the culinary arts in any way, I can recognize that Michael has collected a tantalizing array of recipes from friends and associates around the world. With this collection, you will embark on a wonderful journey through the cultures and traditions of the United States, Canada, Tibet, the British Isles, Brazil, Denmark, Holland, France, Mongolia, Australia and more. And of course sharing our food is a wonderful way to appreciate human diversity while also celebrating our common humanity.

For more than fifteen years Michael and I have had many unforgettable experiences — ever since he first presented the *Mystical Arts of Tibet* on tour in Hampton in 1999. Subsequently he established the tradition of including the tours every year as part of his most impressive lineup of world class performers at the American Theater. On a personal level, we've also been able to share some wonderful experiences (and a few adventures) traveling to teachings by His Holiness the Dalai Lama in venues ranging from Mexico City to New York, Atlanta, and Washington DC, not to mention our pilgrimages to both Drepung Loseling and Sarnath in India.

Michael is a treasured member of our spiritual community, an ardent supporter of the Tibetan cause, and a beloved friend who has brought great love and care to assembling this book. With the same compassion and commitment he brought as an arts presenter helping others open their eyes to the value of all cultural traditions, Michael now uses food as a symbol of community, and how so many of our most memorable and valued experiences and lessons happen in a kitchen or at a dining table.

Thanks to Michael for touching the hearts of so many with his genuine warmth and concern, and for creating this book that will benefit the work of Drepung Loseling Monastery in helping to foster compassion, and to facilitate His Holiness the Dalai Lama's vision for the convergence of science and Buddhism for their mutual enrichment.

— Geshe Lobsang Tenzin Negi

Geshe Lobsang Tenzin Negi, PhD, is the Spiritual Director of Drepung Loseling Monastery and is a Professor of Practice in the Department of Religion at Emory University in Atlanta. He is a renowned pioneer in the science of meditation and the developer of Cognitively-Based Compassion Training, one of the leading protocols in the current scientific study of meditation.

Avalokiteshvara Mandala
The Sand Painting of True Compassion
Photo courtesy of Drepung Loseling Monastery

Among all of the artistic traditions of Tibetan Buddhism, that of creating mandalas with colored sands ranks as one of the most exquisite and unique. Similar to the ancient traditions of Native American sand painting, millions of grains of sand are painstakingly laid into an intricate and deeply meaningful pattern over a period of three or four days.

Based on a centuries old iconography which includes geometric shapes and a multitude of spiritual symbols, the mandala is a powerful tool for meditation and for re-consecrating the earth and all of its inhabitants.

Traditionally, most mandalas are deconstructed shortly after their completion and the sands are swept up, poured into an urn and then cast into a nearby body of water to be washed out into the oceans in a symbolic and all-encompassing act of healing and well-being. This is one of the metaphors of the impermanence of life.

Dedication & Introduction

This book, Dining among the Stars, *is lovingly dedicated to His Holiness the XIVth Dalai Lama, the Venerable Monks and teachers at Drepung Loseling Monastery and all the Tibetan people in the sincere hope that they will see their homeland again.*

Three Novice Monks at Drepung Loseling, Southern India 2008
Photo: MPC

HH The Dalai Lama
in Atlanta, 2013
Photo: MPC

One of the oldest and most revered monastic universities in the world, Drepung Loseling was established just north of Lhasa (Tibet) in 1416. The university consisted of four departments of which Loseling — *the Hermitage of the Radiant Mind* — was the largest, housing more ten thousand monks. Honoring the legacy of this historic institution and with the patronage of His Holiness the Dalai Lama, Drepung Loseling in India and in Atlanta is dedicated to the preservation and study of the age old traditions of compassion and wisdom.

I am honored to be dedicating proceeds from the sale of this book to all of my teachers, guides and friends involved with the ongoing and trailblazing work of Drepung Loseling Monastery.

Drepung Loseling has always had very special ties to the Dalai Lama incarnations, having been the residence of the second Dalai Lama (1475-1542). Communist China invaded Tibet in 1959 and forced the current Dalai Lama (the XIVth — Tenzin Gyatso) into exile. As a result of the invasion, more than 6,500 monasteries and institutions of higher learning were destroyed. Fortunately, some 250 monks from Drepung Loseling managed to escape the holocaust by crossing the Himalayas under treacherous conditions and then rebuild their institution in Karnataka State, Southern India. I was honored to be a guest when His Holiness officially inaugurated the new hall in 2008.

The centuries old traditions of monastic training have thus been preserved and over the years many more spiritual aspirants have managed to flee Chinese occupied Tibet. Now, Drepung Loseling Monastery in India is home to more than 3000 monks.

Drepung Loseling continues to provide a center for both the heart and the intellect and a sanctuary where inner peace and kindness, community understanding and global healing can be nurtured, practiced and passed on to future generations.

Welcome

I am delighted to have you join me as we explore new culinary delights. I did not want this to be a traditional kind of cookbook with altered or enhanced photos of food. Rather, I hope you will find the love, art and compassion in each and every one of the recipes so generously contributed by so many great lifelong friends.

Photo: Alexander Kravets

Also dedicated to Billie D. Gordon

Mrs. Billie D. Gordon (1906-2006) my great friend and the grand benefactor of the American Theatre. Like the monks, Billie had a lifelong commitment to her faith. She and the monks taught me the joy of knowing that dreams can and do come true. Ms. Billie had two lifelong dreams — to dance on a professional theatre stage (instead of the concrete floors of convention centers and hotels where the competitions were usually held) and to live to be 100 years old. I will always be deeply grateful that both of her dreams came true when we honored her on the stage of the American Theatre on the occasion of her 100th birthday in September 2006 when she actually danced, bringing the capacity audience to its feet.

And to the First Lady of Jazz, Ella Fitzgerald

Gloria Coker, *Ella*
Acrylic on Canvas

It was the First Lady of Jazz, **Ella Fitzgerald**, who planted the seed in my mind for the idea of this cookbook — *Dining among the Stars*. That was back in 1984 when, as Founding Artistic Director of the Fine Arts Foundation, I had the great good fortune of presenting Ella in a sold out performance in the 2300 seat Lafayette Municipal Auditorium in Louisiana. Not only was it an unforgettable honor as well as a longtime dream come true to be working with such a legend, it was also a distinct and unforgettable honor to get to know and befriend such an amazing artist. She and all of the other top flight artists included here have taught us all so much.

Dining among the Stars is a celebration of their legacies.

Ella collected cookbooks and asked me if there was a local/regional book of South Louisiana cooking. Remember, at this time in the early 1980's, Cajun cuisine and culture were on a roll to becoming world famous. Humbly, I gave her a copy of *Talk about Good*, (the Junior League of Lafayette's hugely successful cookbook published in 1967 which then went into at least ten printings. A second edition *Talk about Good II* was published in 1979).

In exchange and in a wonderful spirit of sharing, Ella gave me her recipes for spinach salad and chicken salad which inspired me to develop this exciting project over the years. Those recipes take pride of place as the cornerstones of this epicurean collection.

So the *raison d'etre* began to simmer and evolve as I then went on to have hundreds more privileges of presenting on the stage, in the galleries and in the studio countless legendary world class artists, each of whom have touched and influenced our lives in a positive and lasting way.

Grand Opening of the American Theatre June 2000

LEFT TO RIGHT: Stephen Burns, Trumpeter; Michael Paul Curry; Michael Barrett, Pianist; Eric Miles, Dancer (Principal,
Les Ballets Jazz de Montreal); Beverly Hoch, Soprano; and Claire Bloom, CBE, Actress and Mistress of Ceremonies.
The photo hangs in the Michael P. Curry Hall at the American Theatre, Hampton, Virginia. Photo: Gary Hess, Viewfinder Photographic Art

With the publication of this book my goal is to celebrate the legacies of so many legends and
superstars. I am deeply humbled by the support, encouragement and generosity of all of my artist
friends from many different cultures and countries for contributing to *Dining Among the Stars.*

Collecting all these wonderful recipes has been a joyful adventure. I have tried to remain as close as
possible to the words and anecdotes of the contributing artists and I love how the recipes are not all
uniform. I have broken a few unspoken rules (imagine that) especially in naming each recipe and
including the name of the contributor.

Cooking, like all art forms, takes patience, discipline and practice. But once you have mastered
the technique, you can improvise and use your imagination — much like a jazz musician, or, say a
pianist playing Bach. So discover all the layers and colors — remember there are no real hard and
fast rules and many good cooks actually don't use precise measurements.

Improvise but do not compromise and Enjoy with gusto!

Michael Paul Curry

Our Bhutanese Chef who prepared delicious meals for
literally hundreds of us each day at the opening of the
splendid new prayer hall of Drepung Loseling Monastery
in Southern India, 2008.
Photo: MPC

Dining
among the
Stars   *With Recipes From:*

Herman Mhire, *Iris Bouquet, Photograph*

Olya & Alexander Kravets
Dame Cleo Laine
Jenny Learner
Natalie MacMaster
Debbie Ellis Maida
Mike Marshall
Andrew Massey
Leisa Mather
David McCann
John McCutcheon
Evelyn McDonald
Malcolm McKee
Susan Stapleton McLaurin
Paul Mehling
Thiago de Mello
Herman Mhire
Jan Miller
Elisa Monte
Elisabeth Montgomery
Lama Glenn Mullin
Captain L .J. Mumford
Thea Musgrave, CBE & Peter Mark
Rick Nelson
Doris Nicklin
Renee Olsovsky
Ashraf Omran
Maria Paranova
Gary Pecho
Jennifer Anne Perry
Sally Brown Perry
Quartetto Gelato – Peter de Sotto
Carlos Renedo
Bonnie Rideout
Toni Rizzo
Ali Rogan
Felicity Ryan
Jude Schlotzhauer
Dolores Schuyler
Anne Shuyler
Olive Simpson
Vaughan Burdin Simpson
Jae Sinnett
Elizabeth Reed Smith
Yolande deLadurantaye Snead
Kevin & Cindy Spencer
Sherri Fisher Staples
Mark Summer
Olga Supphozova
Maria H. Thomas
Deborah Thorpe
Mads Tolling
Els Uitendaal Vuijsters
Susan & Charles Wadsworth
Daniel Weilbaecher
Shar Wolff
Jeanne Zeidler
Eugenia Zukerman

Nicki Abbott
Nancy Bagley Adams
Maria Ahn Villali
Anon
Eric Alatorre, Chanticleer
Rani Arbo
Gareth Armstrong
Bea Arthur
Robert L. Barnes
Verena Barnes
Alessio Bax
Marc Baylin
Stephen Beagley
Carol Beck
Paul Bergh, Sr
Peggy Blake
Claire Bloom, CBE
Susan Borland & Jim Turner
Elaine Bromka
Debbie Brooks
Caroline Brown & Stephen Neiman
Roxanne Lopez Brown
Chris Brubeck
Betty Buckley
Stephen Burns
Julie Calzone
Kacey Sydnor Carneal
Colin Carr
Bobby Carter
Linda Christen
Gloria Coker

Martha Cordell
Robert W. Cross
Michael Paul Curry
Richard & Liz Curry
Danu
Michael Doucet
Letia McDaniel Drewry
Judy Dugdale
Mick Escott
JoAnn Falletta
Rob Faust
Frank Ferrante
Ella Fitzgerald
Graham Garton & Barbara Howson
Margaret Gimbrede
Vadim Gluzman
Ginger Grace
Liz Greene
Ronn Guidi
Susie Hamway
Charlie Hensley & David McCann
Dianne Hoffman
Miles & Susan Hoffman
Bobby & Heidi Lee Huber
Gil Hunter
Sharon Isbin
Laura Tryon Jennings
Joseph Kalichstein
Justin Kauflin
Ida Kavafian
Chee-Yun Kim

Table of Contents / Bill of Fare

Laura Tryon Jennings
Cherish
Oil on Canvas

Openers & Beginners Please

Appetizers/Starters

Mike's Fried Anchovies

Gareth's Gastronomic Delight – Avocado, Beans & Tuna

Maestro Andrew's Boiled Egg

Rick's Famous Deviled Eggs

Margaret's Granola

Granny Mop's Green Tomato Chutney

Roxanne's Guacamole

Herbal Recipes — Bouquet Garni; Fines Herbes & Herbes de Provence

Jude's Mushrooms stuffed with Smoked Mussels

Southern Caviar

John McCutcheon's Salsa Verde

Nancy's Reuben Dip & Herbed Vegetable Dip

Judy's Tahini / Tapenade

Dash & Dot's Wondergus

Beverages

Thiago's Abacatada (Avocado shake)

Traditional Tibetan Butter Tea

Elisabeth Montgomery's Cherry Bounce

Buxted Ginger Beer

Paul's Chihuahua Cocktail

Jams & Sauces

Michael's Marmalade

Mop's Zucchini/Marrow Jam with Ginger

Mint Sauce

Mike's Fried Anchovies

*Many guests are taken aback at first seeing them,
but after the first taste they dive in and I usually
never have enough for the whole crowd.*

*Because my family is Italian, we had these little fried fish when
I was a kid but only once a year and that was at Christmas time.*

*We now enjoy them year round since we live half the year in the
San Francisco Bay Area where some of the most spectacular
anchovies and smelts come out of the Monterey Bay
and the other half of the year we are in northern Germany
where my favorite Arab market has them most times.*

*As we try to eat fewer large fish in our family, we have been
finding these little fried anchovies just a tremendous joy and the
flour coating is super light. My kids have grown up on them so
they think they are the most normal thing in the world.*

— Mike Marshall

SERVES: 4–6
(ALLOW 3-4 ANCHOVIES PER PERSON)

PREPARATION

Cleaning these little babies is where most of the work is and is probably why many
people are afraid to purchase them. But I've got a system that really speeds up
the process:

First, rinse the fish in a colander to clean them off a little.

Set a cutting board with its end hanging over the edge of the kitchen sink.

Set a small bowl in the sink to catch the nasty bits.

Lay a single fish so that the belly is facing you. The head is towards the sink.
Slice the fish on its side through the head and make a second horizontal cut through
the belly.

As you do this, the insides should come right out without hardly any effort. Scrape
the head and guts into the bowl into the sink.

Sometimes the insides remain attached to the head and just slide right out as the head
comes off and fall right into the bowl. It's a little bit of a French Revolution move actually.

Once all fish are cleaned give them a second rinse in the colander and dry them
with a paper towel.

METHOD

Heat to frying temperature enough Sunflower or Canola oil in a small saucepan to make it about 3 inches deep. (2 cups +)

YOU SHOULD SET UP YOUR FRYING STATION THUSLY:

Set up two bowls to the left of the frying oil. The far left bowl will hold the fish.

The bowl nearer to the frying oil will hold 2 cups of flour

To the right of your cooking oil put a plate with a couple of layers of paper towels on it where the finished fish will land after they are fried.

Take about 5 fish and dredge them in the flour. Mix them around with your hands to coat them. One by one take a fish out by the tail and shake off excess flour and toss them into the hot oil.

When all 5 fish are in the oil give them about 1 minute of cooking time.

Scoop them out with a strainer and toss them onto the paper toweled plate.

When plate is full, sprinkle with salt and some fresh lemon juice.

Serve while still warm….then on to the next batch.

Yum!

Photo: Maria Camillo

MIKE MARSHALL is universally regarded as one of the most versatile and accomplished string instrumentalists. A master of the mandolin, guitar, mandocello and violin, he has been creating some of the most forward thinking instrumental music for more than 35 years. His concert tours continue to take him around the globe. Whether playing with Edgar Meyer, Bela Fleck or Chris Thile, playing Brazilian choro with Hamilton de Holanda, classical Baroque with mandolinist Caterina Lichenberg or appearing with such luminaries as Turtle Island Quartet, Mike is able to swing gracefully between all styles and genres with a unique blend of virtuosity, depth and musical integrity.
www.mikemarshall.net

Gareth's Gastronomic Delight
Butter Beans, Tuna & Avocado

*Simple to make, no cooking required — delicious and full
of good things. I first had this delightful dish, one of my
favorites, back on a holiday in Italy where the
avocados were ripe, large and delicious.*

— *Gareth Armstrong*

SERVES 4

INGREDIENTS

1-15 ounce / 375g can butter beans

1-5 ounce / 125 g can tuna

1 ripe avocado

2 salad onions

A generous handful of fresh parsley

METHOD

Drain and rinse the beans and the tuna. Chop the avocado.
and thinly slice the salad onions.

Mix all the ingredients. Sprinkle with the parsley.

Serve with a warm baguette or ciabatta bread.

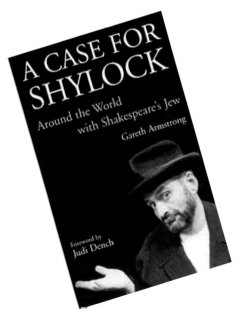

*"Reading Gareth Armstrong's
book reminded me why I like
and admire actors so much. He has
the actor's gift of being totally
serious about his work without
taking himself seriously."*

— *Dame Judi Dench from the Foreword to
Gareth's book,* The Case for Shylock
published by Nick Hern Books

Welsh born, GARETH ARMSTRONG, has played leading roles in most of Great Britain's regional theaters. As a member of the Royal Shakespeare Company he worked at Stratford upon Avon and in London and he has performed at Shakespeare's Globe Theatre for several years. In London's West End he has appeared in works by Noel Coward, Tom Stoppard and Agatha Christie and in the highly acclaimed revival of *Yes Prime Minister*.

For more than a decade, Gareth performed his own solo play, *Shylock*, giving over 600 performances in more than 50 countries.

That is how we met. Gareth came to the American Theatre with this remarkable piece. Subsequently, I had the honor of touring with him when he gave more superb performances in Mexico City and Monterrey, Mexico.

Gareth has been featured in many iconic British TV series including: *Dr. Who*, *EastEnders*, *Birds of a Feather* and *One Foot in the Grave*.

www.garetharmstrong.com

Egg – How To Boil

For the Novice Cook

From the Maestro's "blog" — La Grenouille dans le Fauteuil…

— Andrew Massey

THE GOAL IS TO BOIL AN EGG IN WATER FOR 4½ MINUTES

METHOD

Have the water boiling before you put the egg in. Best to use a small saucepan or you'll be waiting all day for the water to boil but the water must be deep enough to cover the egg completely. No mostly submerged like rocks off the coast of San Francisco, or hump back whales casually passing by. The water must be deep enough, but don't put the egg in until the water is really boiling. Don't let the water be too deep else it will spill over when you insert the egg. Remember Archimedes and Eureka?

If the egg drops into the water even a little bit, it will probably break and quickly look disgusting, like a tiny mammal with a hideous hernia. Yuck. It's a bad enough shock being lowered into boiling water, don't give the poor thing a bump as well.

Have a clock within eyesight. You don't need an egg timer or a kitchen timer or stopwatch or anything like that. Just notice what time it is, for heaven's sake. A clock on the wall might be handy or your watch will do. But a watch is not as good as a clock, because you will inevitably be using your arm for some other purpose when the time comes, so that you are not able to twist your wrist to see what the time really is. A clock on the wall needs to have a second hand that sweeps around so that you can be accurate to within 5 seconds or so. It matters.

Just before you lower the egg into the boiling water, take note of what time it is. Do the math now. Figure out what now plus four and a half minutes is. Then just remember the end time. You can turn down the heat a little bit now. The actual boiling process does not have to look like Yellowstone, which can happen if an egg did crack a bit. Keep it just at boiling. When exactly four and one half minutes have elapsed, take the egg out of the water with your spoon.

END OF COOKING

Incidentally if you want to boil several eggs at the same time, you don't need any more time, just more water. How you serve the egg(s) is up to you but egg cups are a great idea, making the egg sit up proudly to be eaten. A wild unconstrained egg is a bad idea because it is too hot to get a hold of. You'll burn your fingers trying.

It's fun to dip fingers of toast into the egg to soak up the yolk but the most important thing is a really small egg spoon so that you can scrape the inside out without breaking the shell more than you need to get in there. Yum

Anthony Stretar
Hen and Chick
Oil on Canvas
Collection of the author

CONDUCTOR ANDREW MASSEY, British born, has sustained a prominent position with leading orchestras for more than four decades. He has served as Assistant Conductor of the Cleveland, San Francisco and New Orleans Symphony Orchestras and Resident Conductor of the Milwaukee Symphony, Music Director of the Toledo, Rhode Island and Fresno Philharmonics, as well as the Oregon Mozart Players and the Michigan Chamber Orchestra. He has guest conducted the National, Pittsburgh, Vancouver, Iceland and San Diego Symphonies and he maintains an ongoing artistic relationship with the National Symphony of Indonesia and the City Chamber Orchestra of Hong Kong, with whom he toured Italy. He is also a renowned composer — his work *Early Mourning* was premièred in 2003 and his *Violin Concerto, Another Spring* premièred in 2006.

The Maestro and I worked together several times when he was with the New Orleans Symphony. We had most pleasurable experiences and collaborations with pianist Richard Goode (Brahms' 2nd Piano Concerto) and soprano Beverly Hoch in Mahler's heavenly 4th Symphony.

www.andrewmassey.com

Rick's Famous Deviled Eggs

Michael's favorite!

— Rick Nelson

And he is right… these deviled eggs were always my favorite at the annual Glass Guild Exhibitions and at the oft remembered Boxing Day parties. — Michael Curry

MAKES 24 SERVINGS

INGREDIENTS

12 large brown eggs

½ cup / 125 ml Kraft Miracle Whip
(you may substitute your favorite mayonnaise, but I prefer Miracle Whip)

2 tablespoons yellow mustard

2 tablespoons sweet pickle relish

Salt and pepper to taste

METHOD

Bring the eggs to a full boil and maintain until hard boiled (about 10 min.)

Replace hot water with cold (tap) water several times until eggs are cool enough to handle then remove the shells.

Slice each egg lengthwise and remove the yolk, placing the yolks in a mixing bowl Break up the yolks into fine pieces using a fork.

Salt & pepper lightly.

Blend in the Miracle Whip, yellow mustard, and sweet pickle relish, mix until smooth

Spoon or pipe this mixture into each egg half.

Refrigerate for later or serve when finished.

See also Rick's recipe for Tender Baby Back Ribs on page 162

RICK NELSON is Senior Staff Engineer and Group Leader at the world famous Thomas Jefferson National Accelerator Facility (Jefferson Lab) in Newport News, Virginia. He is an accomplished photographer and glass artist and earned his degrees from Michigan Technological University.
www.IgoFoto.com

Margaret's Granola

— Margaret & Louis de Agramente (Monty) Gimbrede

INGREDIENTS

1 pound / 450g rolled oats
(use McCann's. They are the best)

½ cup / 64g flaked coconut

½ cup / 64g chopped mixed nuts

½ cup / 64g sunflower seeds

½ cup / 64g sesame seeds

½ cup / 64g wheat germ

½ cup / 125ml honey

½ cup / 125ml vegetable oil

2 teaspoons salt (to taste)

METHOD

Pre heat the oven to 350F / 180C

Mix all of the dry ingredients in a large bowl.

Warm the honey and oil over medium heat and then add to the oat and nut mixture. Stir together well.

Spread onto a cookie sheet and bake until brown (approx... 15 minutes).

Turn and stir several times during baking.

Store in an airtight container. Serve with milk or yogurt for breakfast.

MARGARET AND MONTE were my landlords, next door neighbors and great friends in Lafayette. Together we worked a large vegetable garden (with Amos Simpson) and shared many a great experience over breakfast, brunch and dinner. Both Margaret and Monte were forward thinkers, far ahead of their times and a great influence on all whom they encountered. Margaret used to drive an old blue convertible (I think it was a Chrysler from the 1950s) but later in life the roof did not work so Margaret could be seen driving down the Evangeline Thruway with the top down but a hand held umbrella up when it rained...and rain it does sometimes in South Louisiana.

The Vatch, Spotted Cow Lane, Buxted. Originally three cottages, the Vatch (surely a corruption of the French, La Vache?) was a "Beershop" known as The Spotted Cow in the 1850's. It was also home to railway workers as they constructed the line from Lewes to London and, of course, as they constructed the impressive Buxted Viaduct which was always a favorite destination on family walks. Mop and Jenny moved into The Vatch in 1953 and Mop stayed there until she was in her nineties.

Granny Mop's Green Tomato Chutney

A wonderful accompaniment for a traditional Ploughman's Lunch, a great addition to a ham & cheese sandwich or as a side for any and all kinds of meat dishes.

— Doris Victoria Milnes Nicklin

MAKES 6 PINT JARS

INGREDIENTS

2 pounds / 900g fresh green tomatoes

1 pint vinegar / 500ml (I like to use ½ apple cider and ½ distilled)

6 whole cloves

½ teaspoon ground ginger

½ teaspoon celery seed

½ teaspoon allspice

½ pound / 220g brown sugar

½ pound / 220g raisins

6 medium onions, finely chopped

METHOD

Peel and cut the tomatoes into quarters. Put into a large saucepan with the vinegar, ginger and the other spices.

Bring to a boil and simmer for about 10 minutes.

Add the sugar, raisins and onions.

Boil for 1½ hours, stirring well and often.

Let cool and then pour into sterilized jars and seal.

See also Buxted Ginger Beer, page 34 and Mop's Zucchini and Ginger Jam, page 37

Mrs. NICKLIN, or Granny Mop as she was affectionately known to the entire family was a huge and wonderful influence in all of our lives. She and Jenny took us all in when our Father died and Mother was in hospital. She later fostered two of our elder brothers and then Jenny (Mop's adopted daughter) and Keith fostered we three younger ones. We all spent many happy years visiting The Vatch where we played parlor games in the L-shaped Drawing Room, played murder-in-the-dark, did jig-saw puzzles and thoroughly enjoyed ourselves in gales of laughter.

Roxanne's Guacamole

This is a recipe my Father (Ismael Arsenio Lopez) shared with Jim, my boyfriend at that time and now my husband. Guacamole was a staple on my family's Tex-Mex dinner table and very foreign to my Anglo-Saxon boyfriend/husband. All of the ingredient amounts are to taste and can vary because the recipe was handed down-by-mouth, never measured.

— *Roxanne Lopez Brown*

INGREDIENTS

3-4 ripe avocados

½ cup / 32g chopped scallions or vidalia onion

1 tablespoon fresh cilantro, chopped

1 clove garlic, minced

1 fresh jalapeno pepper, chopped, to taste

½ cup / 4 ounces / 64g chopped fresh tomatoes

½ tablespoon fresh lime juice

¼-½ teaspoon salt & pepper to taste

a pinch of oregano

METHOD

Combine all ingredients in a cured molcajete or bowl until guacamole is partially smooth and creamy. Serve with corn tortilla chips or as a side dish.

Molcajete — Stone Sauce Bowl (Pronounced "mol-ka-HE-the)
Authentic molcajetes are hand carved out of volcanic rock, and are the traditional implement used for grating spices in Mexico since ancient times. Each molcajete traditionally has three legs, which it is believed, pays homage to the god of the hearth, Huehueteotl, who was associated with the number 3.

ROXANNE LOPEZ BROWN, an accomplished and popular artist, has been teaching art to generations of appreciative young students in the Hampton City Schools for many years. She has also served as a valued member of both the Hampton Arts Commission and the Hampton Arts Foundation Board of Directors.

Roxanne Lopez Brown
Avocado
Colored Pencil

Michael's herb garden, Byrd Court, 2015

Home Grown Herbs
Herbes De Provence; Bouquet Garni; Fines Herbes

Popular throughout the South of France, this is a great mixture which is used in the preparation of grilled meats, fish or vegetable stews or added to green or black olives in the making of tapenade.

I use fresh herbs from the garden so the amounts given are for freshly harvested. If using dried herbs use a little less.

— Michael Curry

HERBES de PROVENCE

INGREDIENTS

5 tablespoons crushed thyme

3 tablespoons crushed savory

1 tablespoon crushed oregano

5 tablespoons crushed rosemary

1½ tablespoons Lavender flowers

BOUQUET GARNI

INGREDIENTS

3 sprigs parsley

2 sprigs rosemary

A handful thyme

1 or 2 bay leaves, crushed. Tie together with cotton string and use in soups and stews and remove before serving!

FINES HERBES

INGREDIENTS

Mix together equal parts of fresh parsley, chives, tarragon, chervil and lemon balm and use in soups and stews.

METHOD

Mix all ingredients together and store in an air-tight container in a dark closet.

Jude's Mushrooms Stuffed with Smoked Mussels

This one is so quick and easy, but it looks fancy and people love it. It makes a great appetizer or party food.

— Jude Schlotzhauer

SERVES 4-6

INGREDIENTS

½ pound / 250g fresh large mushrooms

1 can smoked mussels (you know, the kind that come in a little square can like sardines do)

Horseradish sauce, mayonnaise and Lea and Perrins' Worcestershire sauce, to taste.

Maybe even a little Tabasco or other hot sauce.

METHOD

Wash, dry and de-stem the mushrooms, then place them side by side in a baking dish.

Put a smoked mussel or two in each mushroom cap.

Top with a dab of horseradish, then a dab of mayonnaise. Add a drop of hot sauce and a drop of Worcestershire. Drizzle the oil from the mussels can around the mushrooms into the pan they are in. Put under the broiler until they are hot, sizzling and brown on top. Eat immediately!

See also Jude's "Fried Egg Pie" on page 214

JUDE SCHLOTZHAUER is a fulltime studio artist, with a BFA in painting and an MFA in glassworking. She taught glass working for over 25 years at Virginia Commonwealth University and as a visiting artist at universities and art centers across the country and in Mexico and Malaysia. She currently teaches at the Visual Art Center of Richmond, the Virginia Museum and the Lorton Art Center and is one of the recognized leaders of the contemporary art glass movement. www.judeglass.com

Jude Schlotzhauer, *Peace Keeper, Cast Glass and Metal*
Photo: Taylor Dabney

Debbie's Southern Caviar

— *Debbie Brooks*

INGREDIENTS

3-16 / 425g ounce cans black eyes peas, drained and rinsed

1 small jar pimentos

1 bunch scallions, thinly sliced

1 tablespoon fresh oregano

1 tablespoon Tabasco sauce

1 tablespoon Worcestershire sauce

1 teaspoon ground black pepper

½ bunch fresh parsley, chopped

3 Jalapeno peppers (fresh or canned) chopped

1 green bell pepper, finely chopped

4 cloves garlic, minced

2 cups vinaigrette dressing as follows:

THE VINAIGRETTE DRESSING

1 teaspoon dijon mustard

1½ tablespoons red wine vinegar

¼ cup / 69 mil olive oil

Anderson Johnson
Angel
Oil on Cardboard
Collection of the author

METHOD

Mix all of the salad ingredients together in a large bowl.

Then whisk the vinaigrette and pour it over the pea salad mixture.

Cover and refrigerate for 4-6 hours or better yet, overnight.

See also Brunswick Stew, page 97 and Hoppin' John & Limpin' Susan recipe, page 144

DEBBIE BROOKS is one of the funniest and wittiest people I have ever known. An avid collector of recipes and connoisseur of fine cooking, she gave me this one which is always a sure fire hit at parties and gatherings.

John's Salsa Verde

One of my family's favorites! I got this recipe from my friend, Alejandra Maudet, who remembers her mother, Ruth, making this, although it was never written down.

— John McCutcheon

INGREDIENTS

2½ pounds / 1kg tomatillos, peeled off the husk and roasted

1½ onions, cut in large chunks

2 chicken broth cubes

6 cloves of garlic

½ teaspoon white pepper

½ teaspoon oregano

½ bunch fresh cilantro

½ cup / 125ml olive oil

¼ cup / 60ml white wine

2 tablespoons light soy sauce

Chillies serrano — as much or as little as you want, roasted and peeled

NOTE: I tend to like my salsa with a little bite, so I use 1-2 serranos for a batch this size. Beware! Serranos are not uniform in their heat.

METHOD

In a blender mix the tomatillos, spices, broth cubes, cilantro, onions, garlic and Chillies if you are using them. Blend until all large chunks dissappear.

In a black pan or pot large enough to hold the mixture, heat olive oil, then fry the mixture until it thickens a bit. Add wine and soy sauce, stir well.

Add salt to taste. If the sauce is too sour, add sugar ½ teaspoon at a time. Thicken with flour dissolved in water if needed.

Freezes well!

Photo: Irene Young

See also John's Grandma's Coconut crème Pie on page 206

JOHN McCUTCHEON, a regular welcome guest at The American Theatre, is one of America's most respected and loved folk singers/songwriters. He is master of a dozen different instruments including the rare and beautiful hammer dulcimer. His more than 30 recordings have earned every possible honor and he has produced more than 20 albums of other artists. His books and instructional materials continue to introduce budding young players to the joys of their own musicality. People of every generation and background feel totally at home when John takes the stage with his "little feats of magic" and his concerts have been described as "a conversation with an illuminating old friend." Few people communicate with the versatility, charm, wit or pure talent of John McCutcheon. www.folkmusic.com

Herbed Vegetable Dip & Reuben Dip

*These two dips are always popular
at gatherings and social events.*

— Nancy Bagley Adams

INGREDIENTS — HERBED VEGETABLE DIP

1 cup / 250ml mayonnaise
(Hellman's is best)

2 teaspoons tarragon vinegar

⅛ teaspoon white pepper

½ teaspoon salt

⅛ teaspoon fresh tarragon

½ teaspoon curry powder

2 tablespoons Chilli sauce

2 tablespoons grated onion

1 tablespoon chopped chives

METHOD

Mix all ingredients and chill for several hours or overnight.
Serve with fresh vegetables.

INGREDIENTS — REUBEN DIP

1-14 ounce / 400g can of sauerkraut, drained

6 ounces / 96g shredded Swiss cheese

1-8 ounce / 120g package cream cheese

2-8 ounce / 120g packages of corned beef or deli corned beef, chopped

METHOD

Heat all ingredients thoroughly and mix well. Serve with Triscuits.

A strong and dedicated advocate for the arts, NANCY ADAMS served as the First Chair of the Hampton Arts Commission when it was established by City Council in 1988. She went on to serve as Chair of the Virginia Commission for the Arts and as a valued member of the Hampton Arts Foundation Board. She is a trained dietician, planning meals and menus for the Riverside Health System's assisted living facilities.

Nancy Adams (fourth from left) with other Board members Jim Thompson, Shar Wolff, MPC, Dr. Bill Berg and Nancy Rhode at the Cultural Alliance Awards ceremony.

Judy's Hummus with Olive Tapenade

I always loved serving these appetizers when I entertained guest artists from the theatre at my home.

— Judy Dugdale

INGREDIENTS WITH VARIATIONS

1-6-8 ounce / 283g container of Hummus with tahini

1-2¼ ounce / 75g jar green and black olives in oil and herbes de Provence

Finely chop the olives in their own oil and herbs.

Add to the prepared hummus either by blending in the mixer or simply folding the olive mixture in. Decorate with paprika.

VERSION 2

1-15 ounce / 425g can chick peas / garbanzo beans

1 clove garlic, crushed

1-2½ ounce / 75g jar green and black olives in oil and herbes de Provence

Drain and rinse the chick peas. Add half of the can into the blender.
Add the garlic and the olives in oil.

If this seems too strong, add the other half of the can of chick peas.

VERSION 3

1-15 ounce / 425g can of chick peas / garbanzo beans

Juice of one fresh lemon

Olive oil

3 cloves garlic, crushed

Ground pepper and salt to taste.

Decorate with paprika, cayenne or chopped coriander.

VERSION 4

One 15 ounce / 425g can chick peas/garbanzo beans

One small jar of basil pesto paste.

Blend together and add tahini to taste.

Serve on a fresh baguette, toasted pita bread or crackers of your choice.

Judy Dugdale (second from left) with Dr. Fran Ward, Eric Maddux and Michael Doucet

Dash's & Dot's Wondergus

Growing up with a Mom who was into healthy eating, making her own bread, I never knew what exciting options were out there. I was astonished when I went to a friend's house and they had a grilled cheese sandwich on white bread. I fell in love because, of course, such a thing was not allowed in our home. Dash, who came from an upbringing in a health food house taught me this recipe, and I have used it ever since for openings and receptions, without any guilt of using this concoction they call bread because it is delicious hot, warm or cold!

— *Jenny Learner*

SERVES 10-12

INGREDIENTS

1 loaf White Wonder Bread (if you can't find Wonder Bread, any soft white bread will do)

1-14 ounce / 396 gram tub Merkts Sharp Cheddar spreadable cheese

1-14 ounces / 396g can tall asparagus spears, drained. If you prefer to use fresh asparagus, boil your own but it has to be slightly overcooked to work in this recipe.

1 stick / 100g unsalted butter, melted

METHOD

Preheat the oven to 375F / 190C

Cut the crusts off the bread and flatten each slice with your fingers then spread each slice with the cheese and place one spear of asparagus at one end and roll up loosely.

Place the rolls into a greased baking dish. Brush with the melted butter and bake for 25-30 minutes until golden brown.

JENNY LEARNER is a highly respected, productive and dedicated artist and curator. She currently maintains a working studio and teaches at the Zhou B Arts Center in Chicago. Her work encompasses many media including encaustic, oils, watercolor and batik. She has been featured in many of prestigious exhibitions at Zhou B, Union Street Gallery, the Kol Ami Museum, Swedish American Art Museum and the Chicago Cultural Center, The David Adler Museum, the Union League Club, the Encaustic Art Institute among countless others.

She also runs a successful Bed and Breakfast in the Roscoe Village neighborhood of Chicago… so if you need an enlightening and inspiring place to stay in the Windy City, here it is.

www.jennylearner.com

Jenny Learner
Aurora
Watercolor

Thiago's Abacatada
Avocado Shake

— Guadencio Thiago De Mello

Thiago with classical guitar superstar Sharon Isbin

INGREDIENTS

1 ripe avocado

2 glasses whole milk

Sugar to taste

1 teaspoon cinnamon

METHOD

Cut the avocado in half and remove the pit,

Spoon out the pulp and put it in the blender.

Add the milk and sugar

Mix well. Chill in the refrigerator.

Serve cold and add the cinnamon when ready to eat.

See also Thiago's Picadinho on Page 160 and his Tapioca, page 240
See also Sharon Isbin's Blueberry Mango Pie, page 224

Born and raised in the Amazonian Rain Forest, THIAGO DE MELLO was one of Brazil's and New York's most innovative and accomplished multi instrumentalists as well as a world renowned composer and arranger. After pursuing studies in architecture, he also had a highly successful career as a soccer coach in his native Brazil before moving to New York at the age of 33 to fulfil his dream of studying music. His wonderful compositions preserve the natural sounds and rhythms of Afro-Brazilian roots and Amazonian Indian chants, blending them with an irresistible urban jazz idiom.

Tibetan Tea — Po Cha

*Tibetan tea is actually made of black tea,
butter, milk and a little salt.*

Tea with the Monks on the Guest House Balcony, Drepung Loseling Monastery, Southern India, 2008.
Photo: MPC

INGREDIENTS

4 cups water

2 heaping tablespoons loose black tea (Ty-Phoo, Lipton's etc.)
or 2 teabags

¼ teaspoon salt

2 tablespoons unsalted butter

⅓ cup milk or half and half

METHOD

Bring the water to a boil. Add the loose tea or teabags and boil for a further two or three minutes.

Add the salt.

Remove the tea bags or strain the tea leaves. Add the milk/half and half.

Add the butter and pour the mixture into a blender and mix for two to three minutes.

Serve hot.

If desired add some grated ginger and/or cardamom.

Elisabeth's Cherry Bounce

— *Elisabeth Montgomery*

RECIPE SUBMITTED BY: JOEL LAFAYETTE FLETCHER, III

Elisabeth as the Empress of Japan at a Mardi Gras Ball.

Self-appointed Grande Dame of Lafayette, Louisiana, Elisabeth (always with an S) lived in Southern Gothic splendor until she was 102. She always dressed the way she had as a young girl — most often in a pink pinafore with red high heels and a pink or red camellia in her hair.

— *Joel L. Fletcher*

INGREDIENTS

About 2 cups / 8 ounces / 225g wild cherries

1 quart / 1 good quality Bourbon

1 cup simple syrup

METHOD

Wash and de-stem the cherries and place them in a large glass container. Add the bourbon and close tightly. Store in a cool, dark place for six months,

After six months, strain out the cherries and discard (be careful where you put the discards…see below). Add the syrup.

The resulting cordial may either be sipped from liqueur glasses or spooned over vanilla ice cream.

DAME ELISABETH made this Cherry Bounce using a recipe she got from a cousin who lived on a plantation in Mississippi. Once, while she was visiting, her cousin came to the point in the recipe when it was time to throw out the bourbon-soaked cherries. His flock of turkeys found them, ate them and then they all passed out. The cook, seeing the turkeys lying inert on the ground, thought they had died and decided to pluck and cook them before they spoiled. According to Elisabeth, as the cook got the last feather off the last turkey, they began to come to. It was late November and getting cold on the Delta. The naked turkeys looked very uncomfortable. "Ah know just what to do," said Elisabeth. "Ah went into town and bought yards and yards of pink flannel and Ah made 'em all pinafores."

Elisabeth became a footnote in American literary history as the landlady of John Kennedy Toole, the Pulitzer Prize winning author of *A Confederacy of Dunces*, when he lived in Lafayette during the 1960's. He described the garage apartment he rented from Elisabeth in Conradian terms as "the heart of darkness."

Joel, a renowned art collector, agent and scholar was another of my great friends and associates (and sometime landlord) from Lafayette. We lived in a compound on Fletcher Lane, surrounded by prize winning camellias which his father (the long time President of the University) cultivated. Joel now runs a highly successful gallery and art consultancy in Fredericksburg, Virginia.

www.fc-fineart.com

Buxted Ginger Beer

So refreshing and deliciously tangy on a hot summer's day. This is another treasure I found in Granny Mop's handwritten recipe book from the 1930s. She simply called it Ginger Beer, but I am renaming it Buxted Ginger Beer in honor of the village in which we all grew up. I remember loving to take a bottle with me in my lunch box when I worked as a gardener in Buxted Park and when I drink the ginger beer now it still brings back all those wonderful memories.

— Doris Nicklin

MAKES 8 PINTS

INGREDIENTS

1 pound / 450g granulated sugar

1 tablespoon ground ginger

½ ounce / 15g yeast

2 large fresh lemons

Boil 1 gallon / 4 liters water

METHOD

In a large bowl, blend the yeast with the sugar and ginger until it reaches a creamy texture.

Then pour the boiling water over the sugar and ginger.

Let cool and then bottle the beer into those delightful bottles that have enamel and rubber stoppers and hinge clips.

See also Mop's recipe for Green Tomato Chutney, page 20 and Zucchini & Ginger Jam, page 37

Pound Green Stores, Buxted. Our Mother and Father ran the village general store where we all lived from 1954-1960. The wonderful old house complete with garage and mechanic's shop attached was a grocer's store as far back as 1871 when the population of the village was 1868. Our parents renamed the house Rothley Lodge when we lived there and we also raised chicken, geese and rabbits and each of the six of us had a budgerigar. Granny Mop and sometimes Jenny would babysit, bringing along the chocolate spaniel, Sally.

Paul Mehling, The Hot Club of San Francisco (far right in the photo). *Photo: Lenny Gonzales*

Paul's Chihauhau Cocktail

I was struck with some inspiration — how about a cocktail recipe? I invented this one and (very ironically) call it the Chihuahua. Believe it or not, the grapefruit versus almond taste battle is great!

— **Paul Mehling**

INGREDIENTS

1 shot good quality Tequila

Fresh grapefruit juice

1 shot Amaretto

METHOD

Mix together in a high ball glass and serve over ice.

Under the leadership of superb guitarist PAUL MEHLING, The Hot Club of San Francisco has been celebrating and breathing new life into the music of Django Reinhardt and Stephane Grappelli with style and panache for more than 20 years. To hear the group live in concert or to listen to any one of their 13 highly acclaimed albums is to be transported back to the 1930's and the small, smoky jazz clubs of Paris. This is gypsy jazz at its best.

www.hcsf.com

Michael's Marmalade
with a hint of Ginger

*This is a quick and easy recipe to make and it is
wonderful on hot toast first thing in the morning*

— Michael Curry

MAKES 6 HALF PINT JARS

INGREDIENTS

4 medium sized oranges (Seville are the best)

1 medium lemon

1½ cups / 375ml water

¼ teaspoon baking soda

6 cups / 675g Sugar

3 or 4 ounces / 100g Pectin

A generous handful, about 4 ounces / 100g crystallized Ginger, chopped

METHOD

Peel the oranges and lemon and shred finely. Keep some of the white part and the zest to add texture and flavor to the jam.

Add water and soda to the peel. Bring to a boil, cover and simmer for about 10 minutes.

Cut the fruit into small pieces. Best to work over a bowl to catch all the juices.

Combine the pulp, juice, the ginger and cooked peel. Cover and cook slowly for 20 minutes. Add the sugar and cook for a further 5 minutes.

Remove from heat and add the pectin. Skim if necessary and stir continuously for 5 minutes.

Ladle into sterilized jars.

Mop's Zucchini / Marrow Jam with Ginger

*The trick is to choose an old tough marrow / zucchini
and to boil the preserves slowly for a long time.*

— Doris Victoria Milnes Nicklin

MAKES 10-1 POUND JARS

INGREDIENTS

6 pounds / 2.5kg zucchini / marrow

6 pounds / 2.5kg sugar

4 lemons (use the rind and the juice)

3 ounces / 75g root ginger (tied in muslin)

METHOD

Peel the zucchini/marrow; remove the seeds and cut into pieces about 2 inches long. Put into a large bowl, add the sugar and let it soak all night.

Next day, peel the lemons finely, squeeze and strain the juice and add with the ginger to the marrow/zucchini.

Place in a preserving pan and boil slowly for about 4 hours, until the syrup is clear"

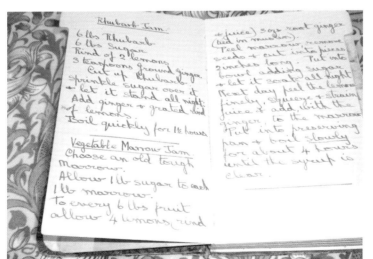

Mop's handwritten recipes. And there is a "lagniappe" (bonus) with the Rhubarb Jam recipe! Try it.

Doris Nicklin was from a family of four sisters, and she was the only one who married (The Rev. Frederick William Nicklin). All four of the sisters dedicated their lives to service for others, in various capacities such as nurses, nannies, missionaries and teachers. Most importantly, Granny Mop (Doris) was a loving, generous and ever steadfast Mother and Grandmother to Jenny and Keith and their family and a loyal, generous and incredible foster Mother and foster Grandmother to all of us Curry's.

Mint Sauce

*Essential when you are serving any kind of lamb dish.
I always have this on hand. I make it fresh
from the garden to last all year.*

— **Michael Curry**

INGREDIENTS

1 large bunch fresh Mint (I like to use Cuban Mojo) finely chopped to make about 1 cup

1 pinch of coarse sea salt

4 tablespoons boiling water

4 tablespoons white wine vinegar

1 tablespoon sugar

Fresh rosemary and garlic to taste

METHOD

Strip the leaves from the mint stalks, sprinkle with salt and chop finely in the blender.

Place into pitcher / jug, add the sugar and pour the boiling water over the mint.

Stir together.

When cool, add the vinegar, rosemary and garlic.

Adjust the seasoning as you wish.

BUXTED PARK is a glorious 300 acre estate with roots dating back to the 13th century. The park encompasses the parish church which we all attended regularly as youngsters (St. Margaret the Queen, built in 1254) the cricket club (which my foster brother Nick Perry Captained for many years) and the newly restored mansion, now listed as a Hand Picked Hotel. The house itself was built in 1722 by Sir Thomas Medley and over the years hosted royalty, movie stars and celebrities. I enjoyed several very happy years there as a gardener during my "gap year" and then during vacations from University. In fact, this recipe for mint sauce was given to me during those times by the head gardener, Tom and it was he who taught me the best way to grow mint is in a large pot because it can be so invasive!

SACRED DANCE, the monks perform an enlightening program of Sacred Music and Sacred Dance. Their repertoire of masked dances includes the Dance of the Celestial Travelers, the Dance of the Sacred Snow Lion, the Skeleton Dance and the Dance of the Black Hat Masters. These dances have been handed down orally to generations of monks for centuries. Dressed in rich brocade costumes, the monks are accompanied by traditional instruments such as the 10-feet long *dungchen* trumpets, drums, bells, cymbals and *gyaling* horns which all add to the exotic splendor of one of the most ancient civilizations on the planet. *Photo: The Mystical Arts of Tibet*

Let's Go! Young novice monks pile into and onto the Jeep which will take them on an exciting outing from the monastery to Camp Number 2 — the nearest village in the Tibetan Colony, Southern India. *Photo: MPC, 2008*

Monks in the kitchen at Drepung Loseling Monastery, Southern India, 2008.
Photo: MPC

Overture & Act I

Breads

Tibetan Flat Bread

Jenny's Very Special Cheese Scones

Verena's Sour Cream Cornbread

Vaughan's Southern Spoon Bread

Intermission

Lama Glenn's Essay & Recipe
For Amdo Tengtuk Soup

Soups

Ginger's Sweet And Sour Cabbage Soup

Joseph's Hearty & Humorous Chicken Soup
(This Could Also Well Be An Entrée)

Jeanne's Harvest Soup

Annie & Laura's Onion Soup Gratinee

Martha's Pumpkin Curry Soup with Lentils

Molly's Ballymaloe Mixed Vegetable Soup

Salads

Elaine's Apple Root Salad

Jan's Caesar Salad

Ella's Chicken Salad

Jack's Cucumber Salad

Susan & Jim's Pasta Salad

Michael's Cajun Potato Salad

Robert L's German Potato Salad

Debbie's Kiwi Fruit Salad

Ella's Spinach Salad

Sides

Peggy's Bread & Butter Pickles

Dianne's Chilli Sauce — Martza

Olya & Sasha Kravets'
Eggplant / Aubergine

Lizzie's Dependable Green Beans

Amos & VB's Grits Soufflé

Susie's Mashed Potatoes

Tibetan Sweet Rice

Eugenia's Zesty Salmon Mousse

Shar's Butter Nutty Squash

Carol's Southern Style
Squash Dressing

Tibetan Flat Bread — Khamba Roti
Traditional

*These staples of the Tibetan diet are usually about 6 inches in
diameter and are either served alone (as in traditional ceremonies)
or they can be served with any kind of curry, meat or fish sauces.
They are especially good with Martza.*

SERVES 4

INGREDIENTS

5 cups / 680g unbleached flour

1 cup / 130g whole wheat flour

Water as necessary

2 teaspoons baking powder

Butter or oil as you go along

METHOD

In a large bowl, blend the two flours; add water gradually until the dough is soft
and pliable.

Cover and chill in the refrigerator for 15 minutes.

Prepare a floured surface and then knead the chilled dough in your hands. With a floured
rolling pin, roll out the dough until it is approximately ¼ inch in depth. Cut into
6-8 inch circles — using a side plate is ideal for this.

Heat 1 teaspoon of butter or oil in a black skillet over medium to high heat.

Place the roti (bread) into the heated skillet. Once the dough starts to expand or puff up,
flip it over and keep basting it with the oil or butter until golden brown.

See also Chilli Sauce (Martza), on page 73

Photo: Dianne Hoffman

Jenny's Very Special Cheese Scones

These are truly delightful and filling, served at afternoon tea
or even at "elevensies" (coffee break) in the morning —
with a strong cup of Ty-phoo tea and a lovely chat, of course!

— Jennifer Anne Perry

MAKES ABOUT 15

INGREDIENTS

2 cups / 225g self-rising flour

3 ounces / 75g grated cheddar cheese

4 tablespoons butter

¼ pint / 125ml milk with a little water

METHOD

Pre heat the oven to 425F / 220C

Mix the flour and butter until it reaches the consistency of bread crumbs.

Add cheese and enough milk to make a soft pliable dough

Roll out onto a floured surface to about ½ inch thick

Cut into 1 and ½ inch rounds with a pastry cutter or lid of a jam jar

Brush with the remainder of the milk

Bake for 10-15 minutes until golden brown.

For plain scones, omit the cheese and substitute 1 ounce granulated sugar.

Jenny and Keith with Nick (standing),
Katie and Tom — my foster family.

JENNY, my foster mother, perfected the art of cooking scones. When the Curry's and the Perry's all gathered together there was always blissful mayhem. Jenny and Keith both handled kitchen duties beautifully (we did the washing up) and were masters at serving meals on a regular basis for 8! What wonderful years and what wonderful memories. Jenny was a Physical Therapist and Keith was a teacher of history (and many other things). Jenny spent two years as a travelling "physio" in Canada before she and Keith married and then moved to Malawi (then known as Nyasaland) in Africa where they spent three years and where their eldest son Nick, my foster brother, was born. Shortly after they moved back to Buxted, they fostered Felicity, Robert and I and then had Katie and Tom...so then we were six or eight again!

Remarkably (or not?) my biological father Thomas Noel Curry and my foster mother Jenny Perry share the same birthday — Boxing Day!

Verena's Sour Cream Corn Bread

— *Verena Barnes*

Verena Barnes on her 90th birthday.

INGREDIENTS

1 cup / 130g self-raising yellow cornmeal

½ cup / 64g cream style corn

½ cup / 125ml vegetable oil

8 ounces / 128g sour cream

2 large brown eggs

METHOD

Preheat the oven to 400F / 200C

Lovingly mix all of the ingredients in a large bowl and pour into a hot iron skillet that has been oiled and baked for 10 minutes. This ensures a crispy outer edge to the cornbread.

Bake for 30 minutes.

See also Sally's recipe for Bananas Foster, page 194

Verena Barnes, known to all her friends as Beanie, was Sally Brown Perry's mother. Sally is a swami and Native American teacher (see bio, page 194). Beanie lived to be 95 and enjoyed an immensely productive life as a farmer having established a self-sustaining homestead in Florida with her Cherokee born husband.

Vaughan's Southern Spoon Bread

This is one of my favorites. It is a wonderful side dish especially for any meats with gravy. Smothered grillades are best — stew meat with a brown gravy.

— *Vaughan Burdin Simpson*

SERVES 6

INGREDIENTS

- ¾ cup / 64g corn meal
- 3 cups / 750ml milk
- 3 large brown eggs, well beaten
- 3 teaspoons baking powder
- 1 teaspoon salt
- 3 tablespoons melted butter

METHOD

Stir the corn meal into 2 cups of the milk. Bring to a boil and cook until thick — about five minutes. Add remaining milk, beaten eggs then stir in the baking powder, salt and melted butter. Turn into a greased 2 quart baking dish.

Bake at 350F / 180C degrees for 30 minutes until set. Serve immediately.

See also Vaughan's recipes (and bio) for Grits Soufflé, page 78 and Chicken Fricassee, page 105

Deeply rooted in the Cajun culture of South Louisiana, VAUGHAN began painting at the age of 10. She studied at the Academy of the Sacred Heart in Grand Coteau and then at Tulane University and the Art League School in Alexandria, Virginia. As she so eloquently says: "I paint the world I feel and see, focusing on the natural environments around me that vibrate with life and color and energy."

Vaughan Burdin Simpson
Lavender Fields
Watercolor

Intermission

Lama Glenn's Amdo Tengtuk Soup
Tibetan Noodle Soup
— Lama Glenn Mullin

My favorite Tibetan dish is a noodle soup popularly known as Amdo Tengtuk. It gets the first part of its name from the place of its creation, the northeastern Tibetan province of Amdo, which in olden times sat on Tibet's border with Mongolia. The current Dalai Lama was born in that region, and rumor has it that Amdo Tengtuk is also one of his favorite evening meals. The second part of the name, or Tengtuk, refers to the manner in which the noodle is made. Teng means to pull or stretch, and tuk means noodle. The noodles are always handmade, using a pulling method rather than rolling and cutting, or forcing through a noodle maker.

There are three main steps to the preparation

1. PREPARING THE DOUGH FOR THE NOODLES

The dough is made much as one would make a dough for any Italian-style handmade noodle. Remember, Marco Polo travelled to Mongolia, not China, and therefore introduced Tibeto-Mongolian noodles to the West.

The city of Khaanbelik ("The Khaan's Stronghold," i.e., modern day Beijing) that Marco visited was at that time the capital city chosen by the Mongolian emperor Kublai Khaan as the seat for his rule over the various states under Mongolian colonization. These included Korea, China, Tartaria, and so forth. Marco thus brought Tibeto-Mongolian cuisine back to Italy, not the fish and rice concoctions that make up the bulk of Chinese cooking. (Of course, because the Mongols occupied China for hundreds of years, the Chinese eventually learned proper noodle making from their overlords.)

As any Tibetan, Irish or Italian cook will know, one should prepare the dough for the noodles sometime prior to actually cooking the meal. This will allow the kneaded dough to rest for some time prior to cooking. I recommend at least 30 minutes of rest time, although longer is better.

One can chose a grind of flour suited to one's personal taste. These days Tibetans living in the West tend to use all-purpose flour. In Tibet, all grains were traditionally ground by water mill, so the flour was slightly more coarse than our Western factory-ground varieties. This gives the noodle a more chewy texture. The rough grind is less processed and healthier.

The dough traditionally is made with just flour, water and a pinch of salt and soda. How much dough to make is determined by how many guests will sit at the dinner table.

After kneading the dough, break it into egg-size pieces, and roll these between your palms into cigar shapes roughly the size of Mohamed Ali's middle finger. Most Tibetan cooks do not add oil to the dough mixture, but instead place a few drops of oil on their hands as they roll the dough balls into the cigar shapes.

Put these dough fingers into a bowl to rest. Cover the bowl, so as to prevent surface drying. It is best to use a bowl that is roughly the right size for the amount of dough being prepared.

2. PREPARING THE BROTH

There is no set list of ingredients for making the Amdo Tengtuk broth. The most common are as follows:

    Onions

    Garlic

    Asian radish
    (i.e., carrot-shaped, rather
    than the round salad radish
    more commonly used
    in Europe)

    Wild parsley

    Wild stinging nettles

    Meat, usually yak, beef,
    mutton or goat

    Salt and pepper

PLEASE NOTE that traditionally Tibetans never add Chilli peppers to any foods during the cooking process. Usually various condiments are offered on the table as optional additives, much in the manner that American restaurants often place ketchup and mustard on the table as optional condiments. The three most popular for Tibetans are soya sauce, vinegar and a hot sauce. One unfortunate result of the Chinese takeover of Tibet is that Muslim immigrants from Sichuan, whose cuisine in recent centuries has been destroyed by the introduction of evil Chilli peppers, have brought their bad culinary habits to the Tibetans, including the terrible habit of adding chillies to food during the cooking stage. For people who hate Chilli for its tendency to obscure the flavors of the main ingredients in any dish, as well as for its addictive quality, this is an evil beyond all other evils.

Amdo folk often prefer wild onions, garlic and parsley to the domesticated varieties. They tend to be tastier and healthier. All three of these grow on the open steppes of the Amdo grasslands, and are often collected and dried during the summer months.

Stinging nettles are one of the planet's super foods, but in the west usually are only available in pill or power form, and even then can only be found in health food or vitamin supplement shops. Again, Tibetans tend to gather their nettles in high season, and then dry them for later use. Because of their stinging quality, one must wear gloves during the collecting process. Amazingly, two minutes of cooking removes the stinging quality. Enthusiasts can easily grow their own stinging nettles in house pots. In the West, the wild parsley is often replaced with Italian parsley and cilantro, while the stinging nettles are usually replaced with some kind of spinach.

Begin by heating the cooking pot and adding your favorite cooking oil. Traditional Tibetans generally prefer animal fat for their oil. They do this by taking a fresh cube or strip of what they call tsilu, the white layer of outer fat on an animal's body, and melting in the pan. Of course any oil will do. I usually use extra virgin olive oil. Finely chop the onions and toss them into the hot oil, along with a pinch of salt and pepper. I personally like yellow onions in my Amdo Tengtuk. For salt, Tibetans prefer the high altitude "Himalayan red (or pink) salt," as it is known in the West. This high altitude rock salt can have as many as eighty to a hundred different minerals in it, and thus has many health benefits. (A teaspoon of it in a glass of water is a common Tibetan cure for a migraine headache.) I usually use a good quality kosher salt.

One wants to caramelize the onions a tad before adding the other ingredients, being careful not to burn them. Once this has been accomplished, add the meat, radish, garlic and any other root vegetables being used. I sometimes like to include potatoes and carrots, although Tibetans tend to think that too many veggies can harm a meat eater's pride.

Sauté all of these for five minutes or so, and then add whatever liquid you will use. If you use plain water, try to get a natural hard water with no chemical additives, such as chlorine or fluoride that will distort the flavor. One can also use a natural beef, yak or chicken broth. Tibetans like to make their own broth from beef or yak marrow. I agree with them, and am not a fan of supermarket broths. Better to make one's own once a month, reduce it, and freeze in an ice cube container. Three or four of the frozen cubes can be added to the broth for flavor and nutrition.

Here I have mentioned chicken broth as an option. Tibetans in general and Amdo folks in particular prefer to eat red meat from large animals. Chicken and fish were considered too small for ordinary consumption. The karma of killing a yak is much the same as the karma of killing a sardine or a chicken. In the world of karmic economics, one slaughtered yak feeds a family for many months, whereas a sardine or chicken barely makes a meal for one person. Do the math, and you can appreciate the logic. Fish and chickens were usually only eaten as prescribed medicines.

Photo: Dianne Hoffman

3. BRINGING IT ALL TOGETHER

Once the broth is brought to a boil, one takes the dough fingers from the fridge and begins the noodle-adding process. I like to sprinkle some fresh flour over the dough fingers, to make them less sticky.

One then takes one of the dough fingers in one's left hand, somewhat like holding a pen, and with the right hand pinches the tip of the dough cigar, flattening it. One then pulls off the flattened piece and drops it into the pot

Repeat this until all the dough fingers have been transformed into stretch noodles and dropped into the pot. Each noodle should be roughly the size of a thumb nail. The thickness of each will vary, giving a wonderful variety of textures to the noodle concoction.

If the soup is being made for a large gathering, several family members or friends will participate in this noodle-making process, each standing around the pot and "pulling" noodles, dropping them one by one into the pot.

Once all noodles have been added, one allows the mixture to cook for five minutes, and then adds any leaf vegetables and herbs, such as stinging nettles, spinach, spring onion stalks, parsley, cilantro, and so forth. If you use soft spinach, it is best to add it to the individual dishes immediately after the soup is served into a bowl. Soft spinach tends to turn bitter when overcooked.

Amdo Tengtuk keeps very well overnight, and Tibetans love to have the leftovers for breakfast the next day, often with a deep fried bread and a side of fresh yak yogurt (well, dri yogurt, from the female yak).

4. A FEW CONCLUDING REFLECTIONS

As well as being the birthplace of the present Dalai Lama and former Panchen Lama, Amdo was also the birthplace of Lama Tsongkhapa (1357–1419), who was the founder of Tibet's Yellow Hat School of Buddhism. He was also the guru of the First Dalai Lama. Amdo Tengtuk is said to have been his favorite food, and to carry his special blessing.

The reason it carries his blessing is that although every noodle varies in both size and cooking time (as we can see above, each noodle is stretched and dropped into the soup individually, meaning that some go in first and others go in later), nonetheless each seems to cook al dente. In the world of noodle cooking, this is something of a miracle.

The second blessing from Tsongkhapa has to do with monastic life. Tibetan monks tend to have Amdo Tengtuk in the evening. Some monasteries were very large, housing several thousand monks, and the cooking pots were therefore large enough to make a large bowl for each of the monks, often ten to fifteen feet across and five or six feet deep. Visitors to Tibet will perhaps have seen the kitchen in a large monastery of that nature. The pot tends to be as large as a room, and has a raised clay platform built around it. The clay platform also acts as insulation to the pot, so that the heat does not escape from the sides of the pot. Imagine cooking in a pot that is submerged in a hole in the ground, with the fire under it.

The monks preparing the meal walk on that clay platform, circling the submerged pot and dropping ingredients into it.

Tibetans like to tell of how occasionally one of the monks would fall into the pot, unnoticed. People would ask, "Where is Tashi?" The answer would only be revealed when the soup was served, and Tashi's cooked body was discovered at the bottom of the pot.

The second miracle blessing from Lama Tsongkhapa is that anyone who dies in the task of preparing Amdo Tengtuk is assured a rebirth in a Buddhist paradise, where Amdo Tengtuk is served every night.

Many Tibetans adopt a vegetarian diet for two weeks out of the year, usually the first two weeks of the auspicious fourth month. When this is done, they will use vegetable oil rather than animal fat, and will use dried cheese rather than meat.

It sometimes surprises Westerners to learn that most Buddhists eat meat. In fact Buddha and Christ were both meat eaters; Hitler was the vegetarian.

Recipe by Buddhist author and meditation teacher LAMA GLENN MULLIN, PhD, an Irish Canuck who lived with the Tibetans for the better part of twenty years. Dr. Glenn Mullin, the author of more than 20 books, is one of the most distinguished Tibetologists, Buddhist writers and translator of classical Tibetan literature. He divides his time between writing, teaching, meditating and leading tour groups to the sacred places of Nepal and Tibet. He studied under thirty five of the greatest living masters of Tibetan Buddhism. Many of his books have become instant classics, most notably *The Fourteen Dalai Lamas* which was published by Clear Light Publishers in 2001.

Ginger's Sweet & Sour Cabbage Soup

Very Easy To Make And Very Tasty.

— *Ginger Grace*

Photo: Kristin Hoebermann

INGREDIENTS

> 1 large head cabbage
>
> 1 cup / 130g raisins
>
> Juice of 1 large lemon

METHOD

> Cut cabbage into small pieces. Cover with water in large pot, with juice of a large lemon, and raisins. Cook slowly for a long time until it is well cooked.

See also Ginger's recipe for Salmon Pecan loaf, page 173

GINGER toured the nation starring opposite the legendary Rich Little in *The Presidents*, in which she played all of the First Ladies of America from Jackie Kennedy to Hillary Clinton. She continues to work extensively in regional theatre playing leading roles in *Cat on a Hot Tin Roof, Doubt, Who's Afraid of Virginia Wolf, Elektra, Dancing at Lughnasa* and *A Midsummer Night's Dream*.

We first met and worked together in 2007 when she brought her stunning one-woman show, *The Belle of Amherst* to the American Theatre.

www.thebelleofamherst.com

Joseph's Hearty & Humorus Chicken Soup

I love to cook, but most recipes I have are copies or total experiments that change from time to time. But here is one that is consistent and does not fail to impress, strangely enough. I say "strangely enough" because you wouldn't think chicken soup is either a challenge or something that can differ from cook to cook. But this, while adapted from Julia Child, is different!

— Joseph Kalichstein

INGREDIENTS

One small chicken (best is Kosher, as they are fresher, or organic, but definitely not large and ancient!)

Largest possible heavy (cast iron or the like) pot

3 or 4 leeks

1 large onion

1 large turnip

1 large parsnip

1 clove garlic

6 carrots

Bunch or handful parsley

Bunch dill

A few Peppercorns (whole)

Salt to taste (be very liberal, if your health permits!)

2 stalks celery

I prefer no bay leaf, but it is certainly okay to add

METHOD

Throw the chicken in the pot (if you have good aim; otherwise, just put it in gently.)

Cut the leeks so that most of the green part is gone and you are left with 2-3 inches, after cutting off the root part also. Make a cross cut at the top, so that you can rinse under very strong stream of cold water to remove dirt and earth from between the leaves.

With all other veggies: rinse thoroughly but DO NOT peel or otherwise get rid of any outer layers: this way you will get a darker, more robust and healthier soup. Unlike the French, I have no qualms about discarding all the vegetables when the soup is done.)

I make a little slit in the onion, garlic, parsnip and turnip, to allow for maximum flavoring.

Put all in the pot and almost fill with water. (the " almost" is to prevent overflow, once the soup is boiling.) Bring to a brisk boil and then turn heat off just so there is a gentle ripple of simmering. (This is the hardest part of the whole process! So you see how simple this is.)

Cover pot tightly.

And here is where I depart from all recipes that I have seen: cook FOREVER! (4-5 hours, like a good Italian sauce!). Once you have it simmering perfectly, you do not have to be around. Just don't take off on a two-week vacation while the pot is on. You may want to visit it and taste half way in, in case you need to add some salt.

The long cooking process certainly makes for a richer soup, but surprisingly, it does not diminish the deliciousness of the chicken itself. I often, after cleaning the chicken, make a wonderful chicken salad with diced raw celery, salt, pepper, and mayo to taste. (Start with the minimum: you will be surprised how little mayo you really need!)

The only down side to the long cooking is that the chicken will be very soft , so you want to be careful as you take it out, so that it does not break apart. But it is worth the effort!

After removing the chicken and all the vegetables, wait till cool, then refrigerate overnight.

When you come back to it, the fat will have congealed as a top layer and is very easy to remove. If you are Hungarian or a very old Eastern European Jew you would use the chicken fat as butter on bread or as fat whenever cooking calls for shortening or the like. I may be sued by the AMA, but I must say that it is incredibly delicious.

What a way to go!

BUT, whether you use the chicken fat or not, it is imperative that you skim it off the soup: without doing that, the soup will be too greasy.

So there!

World renowned pianist JOSEPH KALICHSTEIN was born in Tel Aviv. His amazing international career was launched with the assistance of the legendary pianist Claudio Arrau who arranged for him to attend the Juilliard School of Music. He won the Young Concert Artists International Auditions in 1967 and in 1968 performed with the New York Philharmonic under Leonard Bernstein — a nationally televised concert. He also took the coveted top prize at the Leventritt Competition. He regularly appears as guest soloist with such esteemed orchestras as The New York Philharmonic, the Cleveland Orchestra, and the London Symphony. He has collaborated with conductors Andre Previn, Daniel Barenboim, Pierre Boulez, Christoph von Dohnanyi, Zubin Mehta, Leonard Slatkin and a host of others.

Now a member of the faculty at the Juilliard School of Music, Joseph has also been touring internationally for decades with the Kalichstein/Laredo/Robinson Trio. The Trio has recorded most of the classic piano trio repertoire. www.kalichstein-laredo-robinsontrio.com

Jeanne's Harvest Soup

This recipe was created at the 2015 Chef Challenge by a team from Matthew Whaley and Stonehouse Elementary Schools. It is part of an effort to improve the nutritional value of food served in schools, while also making it tasty and appealing to kids and adults alike. I like to add a jalapeno pepper (with the seeds) cut in half to the pot while cooking to give the soup a little extra kick.

— Jeanne Zeidler

SERVES 6

INGREDIENTS

4 ounces / 100g fresh kale, roughly chopped

½ medium onion, chopped

½ medium carrot, diced

3 teaspoons garlic, minced

2 tablespoons olive oil

1½ cups / 200g tomatoes, diced

4 ounces / 100g potatoes (do not peel), roughly chopped

1-11 ounce can / 275g pinto beans, low sodium drained and rinsed

1-11 ounce can / 275g Great Northern beans, low sodium — drained and rinsed

3 teaspoons chicken base or bouillon, low sodium (dry, not broth or stock)

8 cups water

½ teaspoon black pepper

1 Jalapeno pepper cut in half

METHOD

Wash hands and wash all fresh veggies. Prep all fresh veggies. Sauté kale, onions, carrots and garlic in oil. In large soup pot, whisk base or bouillon and water. Add sautéed veggies, tomatoes, potatoes, and beans. Bring to a boil and then simmer. Add pepper, stir and continue to simmer until you are ready to eat.

As Mayor of Williamsburg, Jeanne Zeidler officially welcomed HM Queen Elizabeth II
for the America's 400th Anniversary celebrations in Jamestown, 2007.
Photo: The Colonial Williamsburg Foundation

Photo: Monica Sigmon

JEANNE ZEIDLER holds the great distinction of having been elected as the first female Mayor of the City of Williamsburg, Virginia (1998-2010). She served as Director of the world renowned Hampton University Museum from 1980-2001 where she oversaw the renovation of a historic building on campus to house the impressive collections and programs. She also worked for the Colonial Williamsburg Foundation (2001-2004) where she oversaw the renovation, expansion and program model for the Kimball Theatre on Duke of Gloucester Street. As Director of Jamestown 2007, she directed events for the 400th Anniversary of the founding of Jamestown. Always active in public service, Jeanne has also served on the Williamsburg-James City County School Board as well as on the boards of the Virginia Symphony, WHRO Public Broadcasting and as President of the Peninsula Council for the Arts. She was a founding member of the Board of the Cultural Alliance and was awarded the prestigious Alli Award in 2010.

Jeanne is President and CEO of the Williamsburg Health Foundation. She has published many articles and papers and contributed numerous books on art and history.

Annie & Laura's Onion Soup Gratinée

One traditional dish I will always treasure is my Mom's Onion Soup on Christmas Eve. My mother was one of those people who loved entertaining and cooking for her family and friends. She was a single mum who raised four children while founding Annie's Book Stop and running 140 franchised bookstores all around the country. It was not unusual for her to work 14- to 16-hour days, but she always found a way to elegantly manage dinners for everyone. The evening meal was the highlight of her day even if it wasn't until 9 p.m. Pretty linens always adorned the table which was set in the early morning hours in anticipation of our gathering.

When my mum passed I painted an entire series in her memory, and she continues to be an ever present influence and inspiration to me. The "Cereal Series" captures the essence of family and fleeting morning moments, rendering simple and quiet images that belie lives that are never quite still. The pretty linen backdrops throughout the series are a gentle nod to her. There are coffee cups, cereal bowls, and assorted found materials used as metaphors to remind us of smaller meaningful moments which sometimes go unnoticed; of reflective mornings; and of fond childhood memories of your favorite cereal. My mum's "joie de vivre", energy, and continuing guiding spirit provides a constant source and reminder to reflect on life's smaller moments and to celebrate at once the simplicity and complexity of the world around me.

— Laura Tryon Jennings

In yet another one of life's coincidences, LAURA and I actually attended the same college back in the UK. Not in the same years, you understand, but there anyway. We met in Virginia and where she was winning many prizes and awards. I had the pleasure of presenting her solo exhibition at The Charles H. Taylor Arts Center, and that show not only broke but set the standard for sales!

"The underlying theme of most of my work is the tension between chaos and tranquility. I love to project a feeling of calmness and peacefulness and enlightenment that hopefully causes the viewer to pause, look and focus on the art and serenity within the moments of everyday life. These are my interpretations of some of life's magnetic moments. Enjoy"

www.LTryonJennings.com

Laura Tryon Jennings, *Sunny Nest*, *Oil on linen*

INGREDIENTS

¼ lb / 125g butter	1 quart / 1 liter chicken stock
2 huge Spanish onions	Handful of parsley
4 tablespoons flour	1 teaspoon of thyme
1 teaspoon salt	1 cup / 250ml dry white wine
Pepper to taste	2 teaspoons cognac or any brandy
1-2 garlic cloves, crushed	Italian bread
1-1½ quarts / 1½ liter beef stock	Grated cheeses: parmesan, mozzarella, Swiss, cheddar

METHOD

Slice onions finely and sauté gently over medium heat in butter for approximately 30 minutes.

Add flour, salt, pepper, garlic. Cook another few minutes. Combine beef and chicken stock in a large pot. Add onions, parsley, thyme and wine. Stir and cook all together in pot on high just until it comes to boil then simmer for approximately 45 minutes.

Add cognac or brandy. Cut bread to fit soup bowls (use oven friendly bowls). After bread is cut to fit, put on a cookie sheet and lightly brown in 400 degree oven. Put bread on bottom of soup bowl. Sprinkle with parmesan cheese. Add soup on top. Cover with a generous mixture of Swiss, mozzarella, and cheddar cheese. Spread cheese to the edge of bowls. Place bowls on cookie sheets. Bake at 400F / 200C degrees (about 8 minutes) or put under broiler until cheese melts and bubbles.

Martha's Pumpkin Curry Soup with Lentils

— Martha Cordell

SERVES 4

I SERVE THIS OVER ½ A BAKED SWEET POTATO

INGREDIENTS

1 small onion, sliced

2 garlic cloves, minced

3 cups / 750ml vegetable broth

½ cup / 64g red lentils

1 cup canned pumpkin puree or roasted pumpkin puree*

1 tablespoon curry powder

1 teaspoon ground cinnamon

1 teaspoon garam masala**

⅛ teaspoon cayenne powder, or to taste

1-2 apples, cubed or pureed

salt/pepper to taste

pomegranate molasses, for garnish***

*please note that canned pumpkin is not the same as canned pumpkin pie filling, which should not be substituted. To make your own pumpkin puree, cut a pumpkin in half, scoop out the seeds and roast, cut side down, in a 400 degree oven for 50-60 minutes, or until pumpkin flesh is soft when poked with a fork. For the smoothest consistency, puree the roasted pumpkin pulp in a food processor or blender.

**optional. Garam masala is a spice mix found in the Indian specialty shops or the ethnic food section of most grocery stores.

***optional. Pomegranate molasses is a syrup frequently used in Middle-Eastern cooking, which can be found in the specialty food or ethnic food sections of many grocery stores.

METHOD

Line a medium pot with a thin layer of water.

Over medium-high heat, add onions and cook 2-3 minutes until translucent.

Add garlic and cook for 3-5 minutes or until water is absorbed.

Add broth, lentils and apple pieces. Bring to a boil. Cover and reduce heat to medium and cook for 7-10 minutes, or until lentils are orange and soft.

Add pumpkin, curry powder, cinnamon, garam masala, cayenne pepper and salt and pepper to taste. Stir to combine.

Reduce heat to low and cook for 5 minutes.

Finish with a drizzle of pomegranate syrup and enjoy!

Top with yogurt, pomegranate seeds and toasted pumpkin seeds.

Don't overcook the lentils...they should have form.

For more than a quarter of a century, MARTHA CORDELL has been acknowledged as an internationally renowned psychic, intuitive healer and life and breath coach. She regularly presents and leads workshops, seminars and individual destiny sessions throughout the United States, Great Britain and France. Martha was also a highly successful marketing professional for several nationwide real estate companies.

www.marthcordell.com

Molly's Ballymaloe Mixed Vegetable Soup

*In the fifty-two (and counting) year history of The Swingle
Singers, Michael Curry is the only concert promoter to have been
awarded the accolade of being thrown into a swimming pool after
the gig by the group. This historic event occurred in Lafayette
Louisiana — and apparently he bore no grudge since it
did not deter him from rebooking us. We like Michael!*

— Olive Simpson

INGREDIENTS

4 tablespoons / 30g butter

1 cup / 130g chopped onion

1 cup / 130g chopped potato

3 cups / 400g chopped root vegetables (2 parsnip 1 carrot my favorite combination)

5 cups / 1.25L vegetable stock

salt and pepper; dried tarragon; half teaspoon sugar

METHOD

Melt butter in a heavy saucepan. When it foams, add potato and onion and turn until
well coated. Sprinkle with salt and pepper. Cover and sweat over a gentle heat for ten
minutes. Add the other chopped vegetables (I prefer root vegetables, but anything can
be used) stock, tarragon and sugar. Boil until soft. Liquidize or sieve.

Serve with splash of cream and chopped parsley to garnish.

Feel free to experiment: practically anything works. I often add apple to parsnip soup.
If you use a green vegetable the moisture content will rise a bit so maybe increase the
amount of potato a tad. Rather than fooling around with cups my ingredients often read:
1 large onion, 1 large spud, 2 large parsnips, 1 large carrot etc. ...and increase amount of
stock if desired.

For MOLLY music has always been an essential part of life. Her biggest surprise of 2015 was being invited (in high secrecy) to form a choir and sing for the wedding of renowned actor Benedict Cumberbatch! Having grown up in Donegal, Ireland, she earned a degree in Modern Languages from Trinity University in Dublin and then a Licentiate degree at the Royal Academy of Music in London. For many years, she was one of the lead singers in the world famous Swingle Singers and Swingle II groups founded by Ward Swingle. Her television credits include guest appearances with The Two Ronnies, Dame Cleo Laine, Shirley Bassey, Nana Mouskouri and the irreplaceable Basil Brush. She was honored to be asked by the *Guardian* newspaper to write the obituary for our mutual friend Ward Swingle.

Apple Celery Root Salad & Celery Fennel Salad

Every time I ask friends for a particular recipe after sampling their cooking, my husband rolls his eyes — because he's the cook. I'm just the cleaner-upper! I maintain, though, that even as a total noncook, I can still collect great ideas. You never know...I might wake up one day and head to the kitchen with fresh inspiration!

Any recipe that makes next-day foraging through the refrigerator a delight gets my vote!

— Elaine Bromka

APPLE CELERY ROOT SALAD

INGREDIENTS

4 Granny Smith apples

1 Knob celery (celeriac) — aka celery root

1 celery stalk

1-8 ounce can / 200g pineapple (chunks, or slices)

2 handfuls walnuts

1 teaspoon salt (Kosher)

1 tablespoon sugar

One heaping tablespoon of mayonnaise

METHOD

Halve and core apples. Dice into cubes.

Rinse in cold water three times, strain and keep in the cold water until use (this prevents browning).

Peel and wash knob celery. Shred, using shredding disc in food processor. Immerse shredded content in cold water. Strain. Repeat 3 times. Strain and keep in cold water until use.

Dice celery stalk.

Dice pineapple chunks or slices.

Mix all together and serve.

Elaine in Tea for Three: Lady Bird, Pat & Betty

CELERY FENNEL SALAD

INGREDIENTS

Equal parts of celery and fennel, very thinly sliced

Loads of lemon juice, olive oil

Freshly grated parmesan cheese on top

METHOD

Just throw it all together and taste along the way!

Stays fresh several days — great for leftovers.

Emmy Award winning actress ELAINE BROMKA starred in the off Broadway run of *Tea for Three- Lady Bird*, *Pat & Betty* and continues to tour this remarkable show nationally. She brought it to the American Theatre in 2009 and it is a real tour de force. Her film credits include: Cindy the mom in *Uncle Buck* and *Without a Trace*. On television she has starred in *Girls*, *E.R.*, *The Sopranos*, *Providence*, *Law and Order*, *Law and Order — Special Victims' Unit* and *Law and Order — Criminal Intent*. She appeared as Stella Lombard in *Days of our Lives* and with Vanessa Redgrave in *Catch a Rainbow* (for which Elaine won the coveted Emmy). On Broadway she has appeared in *The Rose Tattoo*, *I'm not Rappaport* and *Macbeth*; off Broadway she has been seen in *Cloud 9*, *Inadmissible Evidence* with Nicol Williamson and in the world premiére of Michael Werller's *Split*. She has played leading roles at many of the nation's regional theatres. And on PBS she starred opposite Rich Little, playing eight *First Ladies*.
www.teaforthree.com

Jan's Caesar Salad

I have claimed this recipe for almost 30 years and have been asked to bring it to many a dinner party. Truth be told, it was taught to me by my wonderful friend Carol Schramm who was our neighbor and gourmet club member in the 1980s. It's easy to make and the tangy taste makes it timeless — you'll want to call it yours, too.

— Jan Miller

SERVES 4

INGREDIENTS

⅓ cup / 75ml olive oil

6 cloves garlic, chopped or crushed

¼ teaspoon cracked pepper

1-2 ounce / 50g tin of anchovies, drained

½ teaspoon Worcestershire sauce

2-3 tablespoons freshly squeezed lemon juice

2 heads Romaine lettuce

½ cup / 64g freshly grated Parmesan cheese

Croutons

Jan and Al Miller

METHOD

In small bowl, mix the oil and garlic with the cracked pepper at least 12 hours before serving the salad. Cover and keep on the counter at room temperature.

Blend the anchovies to a pulp (I use a mini food processor but have also used a mortar and pestle). Add the Worcestershire sauce and lemon juice and place in a covered bowl in the refrigerator until ready to serve.

Wash the lettuce, dry in a tea towel and tear into bite sized pieces. Crisp in the refrigerator.

Just before serving the salad, mix the anchovy mixture with the garlic infused olive oil.

Toss over the crisped lettuce. And the parmesan cheese and croutons and serve!

Add a crab cake, shrimp or grilled fish for a full dinner. One of our favorite special dinners is a ribeye steak with this Caesar salad. Dinner is complete and ready. Enjoy.

JAN MILLER, CEO of Mellen Street Creative, has more than 44 years of professional experience in advertising and graphic design. In addition to overseeing all the graphics design for the Hampton Arts Commission and the American Theatre, Mellen Street Creative regularly produces award winning work for many other leading institutions including The Hampton University Museum, The Mariners' Museum, Fort Monroe's Casemate Museum, the National Center for State Courts and the ITA Women's Collegiate Tennis Hall of Fame (among many others).

Ella's Chicken Salad

Rich but not too creamy.

— Ella Fitzgerald

SERVES 4

INGREDIENTS

4 cups / 500g shredded poached chicken breast

¾ cup / 100g celery, finely chopped

¾ cup / 100g sweet pickle relish

2 large brown eggs, hardboiled and finely chopped

¾ cup / 175ml of "good" mayonnaise — (Hellman's is the best)

A touch of salt and ground black pepper

METHOD

Mix all of the ingredients except the mayonnaise in a large salad bowl.
Add the mayonnaise gradually until the salad reaches the desired consistency.

Serve with saltine crackers or on soft white bread rolls.

See also Ella's Spinach Salad, page 71

I jotted this recipe down when Els and I delivered lunch to MISS ELLA in her hotel suite when she came to Lafayette in 1984. She loved to have a salad for lunch while "looking at her stories" on the television.

And this, along with Ella's Spinach Salad page 71 were the initial inspirations for this book.

The indisputable First Lady of Jazz, Ella Fitzgerald sold more than 40 million albums worldwide. Her unique talents of interpretation and improvisation made the original (now classic) songs of the Gershwins, Rodgers & Hart, Cole Porter and many others, distinctively her own.

Incidentally, as a postscript, Ella was one of the greats who loved giving — but also receiving. I shall never forget that when I went to pick her up to take her back to the airport, she was carrying the roses I had given her on stage the night before. When I commented that I was so pleased to see her carrying the roses (most artists either left them in their room or gave them to the hotel staff), she said in that deliciously velvet voice of hers: "Well baby, you gave me the flowers and now I am taking them home to set on my table." Magic.

Michael Curry with Ella on stage 1984.
Photo: Philip Gould

Jack's Cucumber Salad

My father has a penchant for inventing raw "fresh-pickled" salads, with vegetables juiced in salt and vinegar and light spices added. This cucumber salad has become a staple at our Thanksgiving table, and is the only vegetable dish that my preteen son regularly requests. It is quick to make, light and salty and tangy. It pairs well with fall vegetables and savory meat dishes, and also works as a cool summer side with, say, tomatoes and mozzarella or a cold rice salad. It is very juicy, so can be served in a small dish, or right on the plate if you're courageous about blending flavors.

— Rani Arbo

SERVES 6-8

INGREDIENTS

3-4 cucumbers

1 medium onion

1½ teaspoon salt (or a little less, but don't cut it way down; it's needed for juicing)

Juice of 1 fresh lemon

2 tablespoons rice vinegar

¼ teaspoon dill weed

¼ teaspoon cumin seed, crushed (or a little more, if powdered from a jar)

3-4 drops Tabasco, (optional)

liberal grinding of black pepper

METHOD

Peel cucumbers, split in half lengthwise, scoop out seeds, and grate with medium grater into a bowl.

Cut the onion in half and slice or dice very thinly; mix into grated cucumber.

Mix in remaining ingredients, pat level.

Cover with a thin layer of olive oil (about 6 Tablespoons)

Let stand at least ½ hour refrigerated; mix together and enjoy.

Harmony, rhythm, incredible songs — these are the hallmarks of the New England based folk quartet known as RANI ARBO and DAISY MAYHEM. Now celebrating 15 years of giving concerts and touring, the band's steadfast brew of wit, camaraderie and sheer musicality leaves audiences everywhere humming and hopeful, spirits renewed. That's for sure!
www.raniarbo.com

Susan Borland, *Sunrise Stonington, Maine,* Photograph

Susan and Jim's Pasta Salad
— *Susan Borland & Jim Turner*

SERVES 4-6

INGREDIENTS

1 pound / 450g penne pasta

1 tablespoon extra-virgin olive oil

1 medium red onion, thinly sliced

3 cloves garlic, crushed

2 medium zucchini, thinly sliced

1 medium summer squash, thinly sliced

12 ounces / 300g fresh cherry tomatoes, cut in half

1 package Boursin cheese with garlic and herb

½ cup / 64g fresh Basil, chopped.

METHOD

Boil the pasta in 4 quarts of water. Add salt to taste and cook until tender. Drain the pasta but keep about ¾ cup of the water.

Heat the oil. Add the onion and cook for 3 minutes. Add the garlic and then the vegetables and the ¾ cup of water.

Cook for 5 or 6 minutes, covered.

Stir in the cooked pasta and then the vegetables and basil until they are heated through.

SUSAN AND JIM, my neighbors in the Wythe area and the Phoebus area of Hampton, both have served as Director of the Phoebus Improvement League/Phoebus Partnership. Susan is also a great photographer as you can see from the above.

Michael's Cajun Potato Salad

This is one of my favorite and ever popular recipes. I adapted it from the bestselling Cajun cookbook entitled Talk About Good. It is a fabulous side dish for a summer barbeque and also goes especially well with boiled shrimp or crawfish.

— Michael Curry

Cajun Country, 1976, *Photo: MPC*

INGREDIENTS

5 or 6 large potatoes

6 large brown eggs

1 cup / 130g celery, chopped

1 cup / 130g green pepper, chopped

¾ cup / 100g red onion, chopped

1 medium lemon

¼ cup /60ml French dressing

3 tablespoons tomato ketchup

3 tablespoons brown mustard

2-3 teaspoons Cajun seasoning
(Tony Chachere or Paul Prudhomme)

METHOD

Boil the potatoes until tender.

Boil and peel the eggs. Separate the egg whites from the yolks.

To the French dressing, ketchup, mustard and seasonings add the juice of half the lemon and mix together into a paste.

Cut the boiled potatoes into chunks and add the green pepper, onions and celery. Add the egg whites. Stir or whisk and then add the egg yolk paste.

If desired add some Hellman's Mayonnaise to hold the salad together.

Robert L's German Potato Salad

*I always loved to serve this at gatherings. The recipe came
from my Mother, an excellent cook, in Augusta, Georgia.*

— *Robert L. Barnes*

INGREDIENTS

4-6 medium sized potatoes

4 slices bacon

¾ cup chopped onion

1-10½ ounce can / 298g
Campbell's condensed cream
of celery soup

¼ cup / 175ml Hellman's
(I only use Hellman's) mayonnaise

2-3 tablespoons Kraft honey mustard

½ teaspoon sugar

¼ cup freshly chopped parsley

A shake of pepper

Cherry tomatoes to garnish

METHOD

Cook the potatoes until softened. Cool and peel. Chop into small pieces and place in a good sized serving dish.

Cook the bacon until crisp in a large skillet. Drain and crumble

Cook the onion in the bacon drippings until tender. Blend in the condensed soup add the crumbled bacon.

Add this to the potatoes already in the serving dish and stir well. Add the mayonnaise, mustard, sugar, pepper and parsley. Stir well with a fork.

Cut the cherry tomatoes in half and garnish the salad.

ROBERT L. BARNES was one of the most loyal and dedicated supporters of the American Theatre, always being first in line to purchase his subscription series as soon as the tickets went on sale. A native of Augusta, Georgia, Mr. Barnes attended what was then Hampton Institute and graduated with honors in 1948. He was drafted into the Korean War conflict where he served for 15 months and then he moved to Chicago where he taught piano in the school system for several decades. A self-described "high-falutin" gentleman, he moved back to Hampton upon his retirement and still continues to teach and share his incredible knowledge and experience.

Robert L. Barnes with the legendary counter tenor
Derek Lee Ragin at the American Theatre, 2005.

Debbie's Kiwi Fruit Salad

This was always the most requested and enjoyed dish at our frequent pot-luck lunches for birthdays and other celebrations. It is another one of those delightfully improvisational recipes — that is to say, use whatever is in season or whatever you have on hand. The glazed nuts are the pièce de resistance!

— *Debbie Ellis Maida*

SERVES 4 -6

INGREDIENTS

4-11ounce / 275g cans Mandarin Oranges, drained

3 or 4 large Kiwi fruits, peeled and sliced

2 generous handfuls raisins

3 medium sized bananas, sliced

2 generous handfuls of other fruits of your choice / when they are available: blueberries, strawberries, raspberries, apples etc.

1-6 ounce / 170g container plain yogurt

1 package glazed pecans (if you can't find pecans, try glazed walnuts)

METHOD

Mix all together and hey, presto, you have a celebration luncheon.

NEW ART 2009
Taylor Maida, *The Butter Churner Project*

Tracy Maida, *Essential But Not Necessary*

DEBBIE is Assistant Manager at The Charles H. Taylor Arts Center. She earned her BS in Psychology from ODU and has raised two daughters, both of whom have earned art degrees. She is a dedicated volunteer to such causes as the Children's' Hospital of the Kings Daughters and she loves "playing" in the garden, growing and tending crops of vegetables and flowers.

Ella's Spinach Salad

This is one of the fabulous recipes that ELLA FITZGERALD gave me and which gave me the whole idea for this book. It was back in 1984 when I had the honor of presenting Ms. Ella in a sold out (of course) concert in the 2300 seat Lafayette Municipal Auditorium. Ella was an avid collector of recipes and cookbooks and we shared many a delightful moment chatting about Cajun and Southern cooking. During her illustrious career, Ella recorded more than 200 albums and performed at Carnegie Hall no fewer than 26 times.

SERVES 4

INGREDIENTS

6 cups baby spinach leaves

¼ cup sliced green onions
(use both the green and the white parts)

3 large brown eggs, hardboiled,
peeled and coarsely chopped

5 slices bacon

¼ cup apple cider vinegar

2 tablespoons sugar

2 tablespoons water

½ teaspoon kosher salt
(or coarse sea salt)

¼ teaspoon crushed black pepper

METHOD

Combine the spinach, onions and eggs in a large salad bowl. Cook the bacon in a cast iron skillet until crispy. Remove from the pan and drain on paper towels.

Pour off all but 3 tablespooons of the bacon grease.

Add the vinegar, water, sugar, salt and pepper to the bacon grease and heat until boiling.

Right before serving the salad, pour this mixture over the salad and toss gently.

Sprinkle the crispy bacon bits on top.

See also Ella's Chicken Salad, page 65

Peggy's Bread & Butter Pickles

I may not be famous in the arts but my family thinks my Bread & Butter pickles are great so I always serve them at reunions and get-togethers

— Peggy Blake

MAKES 8 PINTS

INGREDIENTS

9-10 fresh Cucumbers, thinly sliced (about 2 heaping cups full)

2 small onions, finely sliced

2 green peppers, finely sliced

⅓ cup coarse sea salt

3 cloves garlic. If you use the whole garlic, pierce them with a toothpick so they are easy to remove. If not, crush the garlic cloves.

METHOD

Mix together all of the ingredients and cover with either crushed ice or ice cubes. Let sit for at least 3 hours, but preferably overnight in the refrigerator.

THE SAUCE — MIX TOGETHER

3cups / 650g sugar

3 cups / 750ml vinegar

2 tablespoons Mustard Seed

1½ teaspoons Celery seed

1½ teaspoons Turmeric

Drain the cucumbers and add the "sauce" mixture.

Bring to boil and cook until the cucumbers turn green.

Pack snugly and put up in sterilized jars.

PEGGY BLAKE enjoyed a lifelong career with "the telephone company" and then became a valued professional volunteer, working with the Hampton Arts Commission and Arts Foundation as well as in City Hall with the municipal government and with countless other organizations.

Dianne's Martza — Chilli Sauce

A favorite of the monks when they visit, this is especially good (and almost required) with Tibetan Mo Mos.

— Dianne Hoffman

INGREDIENTS

1 bunch cilantro

4-5 small green chillies or 2 jalapeno chillies

½ cup dried crushed red chillies

2 tomatoes

4-5 cloves garlic

1 teaspoon salt

¼ cup water, if needed

METHOD

Cut the tomatoes and green Chillies into quarters,

Wash the cilantro, and cut off the stems.

Put all the ingredients in a blender and blend together.

Serve immediately with Mo Mos.

The sauce will only keep for a day or two.

See also Traditional Tibetan Mo-Mos, page 150

DIANNE HOFFMAN has been hosting the monks as they travel on nationwide tours of The Mystical Arts of Tibet since 2000. A practicing Buddhist, Dianne spent two months at Drepung Loseling Monastery in Southern India where she attended the inauguration of the new prayer hall, ten days of teachings with His Holiness the Dalai Lama and the traditional Tibetan New Year's celebrations (Losar) when she made offerings to the High Lamas. Dianne is a senior consultant at The Northern Trust Company in Chicago.

Dianne with Geshe Khendrup after he attained his Geshe (PhD) degree

Olya & Sasha's Eggplant / Aubergine

— Olya & Alexander Kravets

INGREDIENTS

3 eggplants about 8" long and about 2-3" diameter or two large eggplants

One bunch cilantro

¾ cup Pecans / 100g (or walnuts) chopped

Vegetable oil

Red wine vinegar

Garlic powder or pressed garlic

salt

METHOD

Wash and cut ends off eggplants, do not peel skin

Cut in 4" strips, ¼" thick or cut into ¼" rounds if larger eggplant.

Layer in bowl with ⅛ teaspoon salt sprinkled over each layer.

Let it sit ½ hour to sweat, to reduce the bitterness.

Coarsely chop cilantro and place in bowl.

Chop nuts, place in bowl. Set aside.

After ½ hour, pat eggplant dry with paper towels.

Prepare a tray covered with paper towel to place eggplant on after frying to soak up the frying oil.

3 Tablespoons oil in frying pan, to begin. Cook over medium heat.

Fry eggplant flat in pan one layer at a time.

Add oil as they cook to golden brown about 3 minutes each side, until they turn clear in color.

Make sure there is plenty of oil. Place eggplant on paper towels.

Then layer in 8" square baking pan.

Spread first layer of eggplant then sprinkle with garlic powder or pressed garlic.

Add the nuts and cilantro.

Sprinkle with red wine vinegar (about a tablespoon on each layer)

Cool. Cover and place in refrigerator overnight.

This will last one week in fridge.

Alexander & Olya at their daughter's wedding at the Williamsburg Winery, 2015

Both Russian born OLYA & ALEXANDER KRAVETS are accomplished musicians — Olya earned her Masters of Music Degree at the Moscow Pedagogical University. After serving in the Russian Navy, Alexander became an award winning photographer and now he runs a studio in historic Yorktown, Virginia. Olya teaches piano and conducting and has served as Music Director of several different ensembles in Virginia. Several of Alexander's photos appear in this book, and I was honored when Dr. Olya accompanied me on the piano when I performed some Flanders and Swan songs at my 60th birthday celebration at the American Theatre.

Lizzie's Dependable Green Beans

This was another great favorite at pot luck luncheons we regularly enjoyed with all the staff. As you can see it is another of those deliciously improvisational concoctions and can be adjusted and adapted as you wish.

— *Liz A. Greene*

INGREDIENTS

Fresh green beans (about a hand full for each serving, if you have a veggie lover, make it a BIG hand full)

1 orange, red, and yellow pepper (depending on if you have them or like them)

2 cloves fresh garlic

1 small onion, chopped and diced

3 or 4 slices / rashers bacon (depending on if you have it or like it)

A handful of almonds, or any nuts (depending on if you have it or like them)

Sea salt & pepper, (any herbs, depending on if you have them or like them)

Olive oil or bacon fat

METHOD

Snap the fresh green beans, leave whole or cut (depending how you like them)

Cut the peppers, long ways, to about the size or smaller than the green beans.

Cut or mince garlic

Depending on a person's preferred cooking method or time; boil or blanche the green beans, run under cold H20, dry on paper towels or

put olive oil in pan, over medium to high heat... put those green beans in pan from the start & cook.

Add peppers, & garlic or onions, salt, pepper and any herbs or seasoning. (I add my seasonings later so they don't burn, while the green beans cook)

Cook depending on how crispy or soft you like your green beans and peppers

Add bacon bits or nuts on top before serving.

Serve, EAT!!

Liz Greene, *Balance Series, Stacking the Dice,* Colored pencil

Multi-award winning artist LIZ GREENE is a native of New Mexico. She moved to Virginia and has fond memories of studying with Agnes Johnson, co-founder of the Peninsula Fine Arts Center. Liz won the prestigious Bay Days Juried Art Show in 2000, and three years later she won a Fellowship to the Virginia Center for Creative Arts. She continues to paint and draw and to exhibit, and she volunteers for various organizations.

Amos & Vaughan's Grits Soufflé

This is a great side dish for roasts, or for brunch to accompany eggs scrambled with cheese, diced tomatoes and bell peppers, or with coddled eggs.

— Amos & Vaughan Burdin Simpson

INGREDIENTS

1 cup / 130g Quick Grits (NOT instant!)

2 cups / 500ml water

2 cups / 500ml milk

1 teaspoon Salt

1 stick / 113g butter, melted.

1 large brown egg, lightly beaten

METHOD

Bring the milk and water to a boil, add the salt. Add the grits. Cook 30 minutes or until desired consistency.

Once cooked, add beaten egg, melted butter, or more milk to desired thickness.

Bake in a 350F / 180C degree oven for ½ hour.

See also Vaughan's recipes for Southern Spoon Bread, page 45 and Chicken Fricassee, page 105

DR. VAUGHAN, or VB as I always knew her, is an acknowledged and respected scholar, artist and author. She and her late husband Dr. Amos Simpson were great advocates for the arts, for education and all things equal. Both of them enjoyed long and distinguished careers at the University of Louisiana, and together with Monty and Margaret Gimbrede, we all spent many a happy day in the garden and in the kitchen.

Amos and Vaughan at the Eiffel Tower

Susie's Mashed Potatoes

This popular dish has become traditional break-fast fare
after Native American sweat lodges led by Sally Perry

— Susie Hamway

SERVES 12

INGREDIENTS

5 pounds / 2.25kg Yukon potatoes

2 sticks / 255g butter

1 container parmesan cheese

Small amount of milk

5 or 6 bouillon cubes (one for each cup of water) chicken or vegetable

Pepper to taste

METHOD

Peel the potatoes and cut into squares. Put water in the pot to boil and count how many cups you used just to cover the potatoes. Add one Bouillon cube for each cup of water. Boil until the potatoes are soft and fall apart with a fork.

Drain out all but ¼ of the potato water, reserving this in a bowl.

Add butter and pepper. Using an electric mixer, blend and mash the potatoes.

Add a small amount of milk and mix

Add the cheese; Add more potato water; Add cheese.

If the potatoes are runny add more cheese. Taste — no salt required because the bouillon cubes have salt.

Pour the potatoes into a large baking tin.

Put in oven to reheat.

Make sure you are feeling love as you make the potatoes.

Enjoy.

SUSIE HAMWAY in addition to being an accomplished artist, is a Science of Mind Minister, a Reiki Master and teacher.

Susie Hamway
Bird of Passion

Tibetan Sweet Rice — Dresil
Traditional

This delicious dish is traditionally prepared to celebrate special occasions such as weddings, religious festivities and holidays, especially Losar (The Tibetan New Year).

In Tibet, dresil is made with rice, raisins, a wild root called droma (which resembles a miniature sweet potato) and butter from the female Yak (dri). Since droma is rather difficult to find outside of Tibet, our recipe subsitutes nuts for the droma and cow butter for the dri.

SERVES 4-6

COURTESY OF THE INTERNATIONAL CAMPAIGN FOR TIBET

INGREDIENTS

2 cups / 260g cooked Basmati rice

6 tablespoons / 75g unsalted butter

4 tablespoons sugar

½ cup / 64g unsalted cashews (or any other nuts of your choice)

1 cup / 130g raisins

Additional dried fruits or nuts may be added, depending upon your taste.

METHOD

Mix the butter and sugar into the cooked rice while it is still hot. Then fold in the dried fruits and nuts.

Serve warm with sweet tea or butter tea.

See also ICT's recipe for Traditional Mo-Mos, page 150

Founded in 1988, the International Campaign for Tibet is a nonprofit organization, chaired by Richard Gere, which works to promote human rights and democratic freedoms of the peoples of Tibet. ICT's firm belief is that the survival of Tibet's ancient cultural traditions and wisdom are of profound importance to the global community.

www.savetibet.org

Pouring the sands. A brief ceremony involving chanting with traditional instrumental accompaniment precedes the actual pouring of the sands from the mandala into the water. Along with the sands, the monks pour a little milk and drop some flowers into the water as well. The flowers and the milk, again very symbolic, are taken from the shrine or altar behind the mandala which the monks (or lamas) have constructed over a four day period. Many people bring flowers and fruit to be placed on the altar during the monks' residency.

Eugenia's Zesty Salmon Mousse

This easy to make dish can be served as a dip or as a spread on black bread. I sent my kids to school with these mousse sandwiches and they loved 'em.

— Eugenia Zukerman

INGREDIENTS

1 packet / 3 ounces / 75g plain gelatin

Juice of ½ lemon

1 small onion chopped

½ cup / 125ml boiling water

1-16 ounce can / 450g salmon
(splurge on an expensive can, as it were)

½ cup / 125ml low-fat mayonnaise

1 cup / 250ml plain yogurt
(whatever percentage you wish)

1 teaspoon white horseradish
sauce, drained

Fresh dill to taste

Salt and pepper to taste

½ teaspoon Curry powder
(optional but really you need this)

Photo: Angela Jimenez

METHOD

Combine and process in blender the gelatin, lemon juice, onion and water

Add salmon and fold in until thoroughly mixed together.

Pour this mixture into a bowl and add the mayonnaise, yogurt, horseradish, dill, salt and pepper and curry.

Transfer to a pretty bowl and put in fridge and serve when thoroughly chilled.

EUGENIA ZUKERMAN is one of those rather rare Renaissance women. She is an internationally renowned flutist, artistic director, author and journalist. Recognized with an Emmy nomination, she created more than 300 portraits as the Arts Correspondent for *CBS Sunday Morning*. Her in-depth interview subjects included such greats as Dame Maggie Smith, Leontyne Price, Mikhail Baryshnikov and a whole host of others. Genie and I had the pleasure of working together and forming a long lasting friendship back in 1984. We then collaborated again in 2004, 2005 and 2012.
www.eugeniazukerman.com

Shar's Nutty Butter Squash

A great dish for Thanksgiving or any other celebration.

— Shar Wolff

INGREDIENTS

2 large butternut squash

½ cup / 64g brown sugar

⅔ cup / 75g pecans (I use halves and break most of them up into pieces)

A generous splash of vanilla (I use real Mexican vanilla)

Ground sea salt

½ cup / 64g uneven sized graham cracker crumbs (Use whole ones and make them yourself by crushing in your hands, or put them in a baggie and roll over them with a rolling pin or a glass)

⅔ cup / 160g butter

OPTIONAL: ½ cup / 125ml fresh, whole cranberries

METHOD

Cut squash into halves and steam until soft. Scrape the soft squash from the shell and put it into a baking dish. Add the sugar, half of the graham cracker crumbs, most of the nuts, vanilla, a couple of twists of the grinder of salt, and a bit more than half of the butter. Mix well. Sprinkle the top with the remaining graham cracker crumbs, pecan halves, and little dots of the remaining butter. Bake at 350F / 180C until thoroughly heated.

FOR VARIETY: Try using cinnamon graham crackers

OPTIONAL: Boil cranberries in a small amount of water in a skillet (until they pop). Stir in enough brown sugar to glaze and coat the cranberries, and make them syrupy. Stir that into the squash before adding the toppings.

SHAR WOLFF served as a Military Photographer in the US Air Force. She then earned her Bachelor's Degree from the School of the Art Institute of Chicago and her Master's from the University of Arizona. Throughout her career she has been an exhibiting artist and served as Chair of the Photography and Visual Arts Communications Department at Thomas Nelson Community College for 17 years. She served on the Hampton Arts Commission for six years, her final two of them as Chair, and as Assistant Dean of Technology, Arts and Professional Studies at Northern Essex Community College in Massachusetts.

Shar Wolff
The American Theatre, 2010, Photograph

Carol's Southern Style Squash Dressing

This is usually served as a side dish to turkey or pork roast and it is yummy. You can also add chopped up leftover turkey to it and then it becomes turkey dressing casserole.

— Carol Beck

INGREDIENTS

1 skillet of cooked cornbread (or one 8" x 8" pan)

2 cups / 250g bread crumbs (anything you have on hand will do)

1-1½ cups / 300ml chicken broth

4 cups / about 520g yellow summer squash — sliced thinly

½ cup / 125g butter

½ cup / 64g each chopped onion and celery

1-10½ ounce / 298g condensed cream of chicken soup, undiluted

2 large brown eggs beaten

1 teaspoon fresh sage

½ teaspoon pepper

1 teaspoon rosemary

METHOD

Preheat the oven to 350F/180C

Prepare the corn bread, cool and crumble into a large bowl; set aside.

In a large saucepan, bring ½ cup of the chicken broth to a boil.

Add the squash; cook, covered, for 3-5 minutes or until crisp-tender. Meanwhile, in a large skillet, melt butter. Add the onion and celery; sauté until tender.

Add vegetable mixture and squash/stock mixture to the corn bread.

In a small bowl, combine the soup, ½ cup of chicken broth, sage, rosemary and pepper; add to corn bread and stir until blended. Add the beaten eggs. If it seems too dry, add a little more broth, the consistency should be similar to cornbread batter. Transfer to a greased 11" x 7" baking dish.

Bake, uncovered, for approximately 50 minutes or until golden brown.

Carol with His Holiness the Dalai
Lama (above) and interviewing
President Jimmy Carter

CAROL is the Assistant Director of Programs at the Emory-Tibet Partnership where she spearheads
program development, marketing and outreach. She graduated from Rhodes College with a duel
BA in Psychology and Theatre and Media Arts and then with an MFA from the School of Film at Ohio
University. Prior to joining Emory, she enjoyed a highly successful career for more than 20 years as a
video producer writer and project manager, working on five continents.

Gloria Coker
Planning the Menu
Acrylic on Canvas

www.gloriacokerfineart.com

Act II

Entrées

Jazzy Jae's ANDOUILLE SAUSAGE & BLACK EYED PEA STEW

Ida's AROMATIC ARMENIAN AUBERGINE/ EGGPLANT CASSEROLE

Chee-Yun Kim's KOREAN BBQ BEEF

Marc Baylin's BRAVO BOLOGNESE

Fabian's CHICKEN with SAGE & PEAS

Kacey's VERY QUICK BRUNSWICK STEW

The Countess' BRUNSWICK STEW

Alessio's BUCATINI all' AMATERICANA

Claire's CHICKEN with PERNOD

Olga's Nannie's CHICKEN & POTATOES

VB'S Louisiana CHICKEN FRICASSEE

Chris' CHICKEN MARBELLA

Toni's LEMON CHICKEN with CAPERS & HEARTS of PALM

Natalie's FAVORITE CHICKEN POT PIE

Maria's CHICKEN ROULER

Dolores' CAJUN RICE DRESSING

Felicity's CORNISH PASTIES

Ali's COPPER COUNTY PASTIES

Imperial DEVILED CRAB

David & Charlie's THAI GREEN CURRY CRAB CAKES

Els' CONFIT of DUCK

Rob's ENCHILADAS PERFECTOS

Richard & Liz's FISH CURRY

Dame Cleo's ACE FISH PIE

Anne's FRENCH BEEF STEW

Mads' TRADITIONAL DANISH FRIKADELLER

Evelyn's HAMBURGER STEAK

Gary's BLACK BEAN Chilli

Michael Doucet's JAMMIN' JAMBALAYA

Bea Arthur's LUSCIOUS LEG of LAMB

Renee's LASAGNA for the LAMAS

Susan's RED & WHITE LASAGNA

Low Country HOPPIN' JOHN & LIMPIN' SUSAN

Herman's MACARONI & CHEESE

Olga's MAC & CHEESE

DEVILED MACKEREL

Chef Bobby's MEATLOAF

TRADITIONAL TIBETAN MO-MOS

Ashraf's MOUSSAKA

Graham & Barbara's MUSHROOM SURPREEZE

Frank's PENNE PASTA

Mark's PASTA PUTTANESCA

Quartetto's SICILIAN PASTA

PICADINHO à la THIAGO

Ricky's TENDER BABY BACK RIBS

Trumpeter's PORK TENDERLOIN with GRILLED FIGS

Elisa's RICOTTA RAVIOLI

Ronn's RISOTTO a la PARMIGINA

Maria Ahn's NO FRILLS SAFFRON RISOTTO

Yolande's CRABMEAT QUICHE & DIJON QUICHE LORRAINE

Ginger's SALMON LOAF with PECANS

Alessio's SEA URCHIN SPAGHETTI

Captain Les' TOAD IN THE HOLE

Julie's ZUCCHINI BAKE

Justin's TONKATSU

Jazzy Jae's Andouille Sausage & Black Eyed Pea Stew

A New Year's Eve / New Year's Day Mainstay
for good luck in the coming year.

— *Jae Sinnett*

SERVES 4-6

INGREDIENTS

2 teaspoons Konriko or other Cajun seasoning (Tony Chachere, Paul Prudhomme)

1 tablespoon flour

1 tablespoon olive oil

1 cup / 130g finely chopped yellow onion

1 teaspoon crushed red pepper

2 bay leaves, crushed

3 cloves garlic, peeled and minced

2 stalks celery, finely chopped

1 small green bell pepper, seeded and diced

3-14½ ounce / 411g cans chicken broth

3 or 4 andouille sausages diced into small pieces

1-15 ounce can diced tomatoes with juice

2 cups black eyed peas

Pinch of salt and ½ teaspoon black pepper

METHOD

Remember, there is salt in the broth and in the Cajun seasoning, so be careful here.

In a large black saucepan, heat the oil over medium heat. Add the sausage and sauté uncovered for 3 minutes. Add the onion and sauté for a further 3 minutes, stirring all the time.

Add the celery and bell pepper, cover and cook for five minutes, stirring occasionally. Then add the garlic and cook for another minute.

Sprinkle on the Cajun seasoning and flour, stir well and cook for one minute. Add the broth and tomatoes. Cook for 5 minutes, stirring occasionally. Add the black eyed peas.

Place in a larger pan and cook over medium-low heat for about 30 minutes, stirring often. Add the salt and pepper to taste.

Add more broth if needed but do not make it too runny or too dry. Adjust seasonings if necessary and serve over rice.

Photo: Mark Robbins

A man of vision and great talent, master drummer Jae Sinnett has been a mainstay of the jazz scene from almost three decades. As a drummer, composer and band leader he has produced 14 recordings and has written more than 150 compositions including the scores of five documentary features, one of which *John Biggers: Stories of Illumination* was aired on PBS nationwide. His longtime dream of performing with his Trio and the Virginia Symphony orchestra came to fruition last year — to great reviews.

Jae is approaching his 26th year as jazz producer and on-air host for NPR Affiliate WHRV FM in Norfolk, Virginia. His instruments of choice are Sonor Designer Delite Series Drums and Sabian Cymbals.

www.jaesinnett.com

Ida's Aromatic Armenian Aubergine / Eggplant

This vegetarian recipe is one I learned from my mom (the world's greatest cook bar none) even though I had to sneak peeks since she was always telling me to practice instead of helping or watching her cook.

— Ida Kavafian

SERVES 6

INGREDIENTS

2 medium eggplants, firm, dark and not too heavy

Olive oil

1-8 ounce / 227g can tomato sauce or even better, ½ container of Parmalat chopped tomatoes

2 fresh tomatoes

2-3 cloves chopped garlic

2 tablespoons (or to taste) balsamic vinegar (wine vinegar is also fine)

1-6 ounces / 170g container plain yogurt

Oregano to taste (just a bit)

Salt

Pepper

METHOD / DIRECTIONS

Wash, then peel 3 strips lengthwise down the eggplant, creating a striped effect. Slice into ½ inch pieces and salt both sides, placing on paper towels to soak up moisture. Leave for about 45 minutes, turning over a few times, changing paper towels if needed.

While eggplant is "sweating", sauté garlic in olive oil in medium pan until lightly brown. Add fresh tomato, salt and pepper to taste, and cook over medium low heat for about 5 minutes. Add tomato sauce, bring to a boil and simmer for another 8 minutes or so. Add vinegar and let simmer for 1-2 minutes, just until flavors blend. Let cool.

Preheat broiler. Place eggplant slices in single layer in a large broiling pan or cookie sheet and brush both sides with olive oil. Place under broiler and cook until evenly light to medium brown. Turn and broil other side. Although eggplant can be fried, I prefer broiling, since it absorbs less oil. Let cool slightly.

In a serving platter, place a single layer of eggplant, spoon yogurt on top to almost cover each individual piece, then tomato sauce to cover well. Layer until you have used up the eggplant. The top layer should be the sauce. Serve at room temperature. One of the advantages of this recipe is that it can be made long ahead of time and kept at room temperature, or even the day before and refrigerated. Be sure to let it adjust to room temperature for at least an hour before serving, if that is the case. Enjoy!

Ida with Ms. Billie (as in Holiday).
Photo: Bernard Minditch

One of today's most talented and versatile artists, violinist IDA KAVAFIAN enjoys an international reputation as a recitalist, chamber musician and soloist with major orchestras around the world. For more than a quarter of a century she has been Artistic Director of the *Music from Angel Fire Festival* in New Mexico. As the Kavafian Duo she and her sister Ani electrify audiences in oftentimes daring repertoire. Ida is also a founding member of The Chamber Music Society of Lincoln Center, a founding member of the legendary chamber ensemble, TASHI, and she regularly appears as a guest artist and records with such famous groups as the Orion, Guarneri, American and Shanghai Quartets. For six years she toured the world with the Beaux Arts Trio.

Born in Turkey of Armenian parents, she and her family moved to the United States when she was three. She currently serves on the faculty at the Curtis Institute, the Juilliard School of Music and the Bard College Conservatory.

Ida and I first worked together when she won the Young Concert Artists International Auditions back in 1976. We have worked together many times since.

Ida and her husband, renowned violist Steven Tenenbom, have also found much success in the breeding, training and showing of prize winning Vizsla dogs.

http://www.musicfromangelfire.org/

Chee-Yun's Korean Barbeque Beef

*Short rib meat comes as long thick strips in the butcher's section
of the store. I like to cut them in smaller strips and make a few
crisscross slits on the meat for the marinade to soak in.*

— *Chee-Yun Kim*

SERVES 5-8

(DEPENDING ON HOW HUNGRY THEY ARE)

INGREDIENTS

3 pounds / 1.35kg boneless short ribs

FOR MARINADE

½ cup / 64g crushed kiwi or pear

½ cup / 64g onion purée

10 cloves garlic, minced

1 heaping tablespoon ground ginger

6 tablespoons soy sauce

3 tablespoons gochujang (Korean spicy red pepper paste, which you can get from a
Korean grocery store.) It's an optional ingredient. I personally like to add it to give
a little kick!

6 tablespoons brown sugar

a few pinches of ground black pepper

2 tablespoons toasted sesame oil

METHOD

Mix all the marinade ingredients together in a bowl

Add the beef and mix well

You can grill, pan-fry or BBQ right after, but it is better if you can marinate for at least an
hour (or more) in the fridge before cooking.

Korean born violinist CHEE-YUN is acclaimed for her flawless technique, dazzling artistry and charismatic stage presence. She has carved out a unique place for herself in the world of classical music and she continues to enrapture audiences around the world. She won the Young Concert Artists International Auditions in 1989 and her career has been stellar ever since. She regularly appears with the major conductors and orchestras in the world and at leading arts festivals while continuing to garner the highest praise for her ever increasing catalogue of recordings. Her album, *Serenata Notturno* on the Decca / Korea label went platinum (selling more than a million copies) within six months of its release.

The combination/duo of Chee-Yun and famed Irish pianist Barry Douglas was truly an unforgettable concert experience when I presented them in 2004.

www.chee-yun.net

Marc's Bravo Bolognese

You can do this in your sleep. This is my classic meat sauce which is great served over any kind of pasta that can stand up to it

— Marc Baylin

SERVES 6-8

INGREDIENTS

I pound / .45kg ground beef (95-97%lean)

6 cloves chopped garlic

1 medium yellow onion, chopped

2 carrots sliced into small pieces

6 tablespoons olive oil

1-64 / ounce can (Rotel) organic crushed tomatoes

1 tablespoon organic tomato paste

1 tablespoon oregano

1 tablespoon basil

¼ tablespoon pepper

½ tablespoon kosher coarse salt

½ tablespoon sugar

¼ tablespoon ground cinnamon

METHOD

In a deep pot, warm the olive oil and cook over medium to high heat for about a minute. Add the onion and garlic and cook for another 5 minutes. Stir regularly to make sure the oil coats the onion and garlic. Add the carrots and cook for another minute.

Add the ground beef and brown on high heat until all the pink has disappeared. Stir in the remainder of the ingredients and simmer over low heat for 45-60 minutes.

Stir occasionally. The longer it simmers, the richer the flavor.

Serve and enjoy. Any leftovers can be frozen.

As President and Founder of Baylin Artists Management, MARC BAYLIN has almost three decades' experience in artists' management & career development, presenting and facilitating/directing special events. He has served as President of the North American Performing Arts Management Association and on the Boards of many other leading organizations.

His impressive and loyal roster of artists includes many favorites including: The Aquila Theatre Company, Turtle Island Quartet, Danu, Rani Arbo & Daisy Mayhem, The Hot Club of San Francisco and Flamenco Vivo. Well, heck, I had the pleasure of working with virtually all of the artists on Marc's roster!
www.baylinartists.com

Fabian's Chicken with Sage & Peas

*I found this receipt in an old American RedCross
cookbook. I've tried it many times and it never fails.
It's so quick and easy. Thanks Fabian!*

— Debbie Brooks

SCALOPPINE DI POLLO AL PISSELLI

SERVES 4

INGREDIENTS

1 pound / 450g boneless,
skinless chicken breasts

Salt and fresh ground black pepper

2 tablespoons butter

2 tablespoons olive oil

12 fresh sage leaves

1 cup / 128g partially thawed frozen peas

½ tablespoon fresh lemon juice

METHOD

Cut the chicken into 4 equal portions. Place between 2 sheets of plastic wrap or wax
paper and then pound to ¼" thickness. Sprinkle both sides of the chicken with salt
and pepper.

Melt the butter and olive oil in a large
black skillet. Add the chicken and sage
and cook on each side until golden
brown. Remove the chicken from the
pan and keep warm.

Add the peas and lemon juice to the
pan and stir.

Cover and cook on low heat for five
minutes. Return the chicken to the pan,
turning until heated all the way through.

Fabian Forté was a teen idol of the 1950s
and 60s and he attained nationwide fame
after performing several times on *American
Bandstand* and consistently reaching the
top Billboard listings.

Kacey's Very Quick Gloucester Brunswick Stew

No one will ever know that you have not spent all day making this!
— *Kacey Sydnor Carneal*

SERVES 6

INGREDIENTS

2-20 ounce / 566g cans of
Brunswick stew (Mrs. Fearnow's is best)

2-14½ ounce / 396g cans diced tomatoes

1-8 ounce / 226 can of corn

5 tiny new potatoes, quartered

1-1½ cups / 190g cooked chicken, diced

1 teaspoon fines herbes

METHOD

Mix all ingredients together.
Bring to a boil over medium heat.

Serve hot with croissants.

Delicious!

Kacey Sydnor Carneal, *My Friends have made the Story of my Life*, Acrylic

See also Kacey's Harlequin Pinwheels, page 216 & Shoo Fly Pie, page 238

An immensely popular and successful folk artist, KACEY SYDNOR CARNEAL works eight hours per day in her studio in an 18th century farmhouse in Virginia. Self-taught, she is widely known for her unique and distinctive use of the frame, letting it act as an extension of the painting itself or simply adding an accent to her work. Kacey has been featured in juried exhibitions in 52 cities, 23 states as well as in Holland and her art is in the permanent collections of many esteemed galleries/museum and private collections.

She is represented by the American Oh Yes! Gallery in Hilton Head, San Francisco and Washington D.C and by the Ginger Young Gallery in Chapel Hill, NC and the Shooting Star Gallery in Suffolk, VA.

The Countess' Brunswick Stew

— *Countess Skoorb / aka Debbie Brooks*

Anthony Stretar
The Rooster
Oil on Canvas
Collection of
the author

SERVES 4-6

INGREDIENTS

3-4 pounds / 150g chicken

1 onion, quartered and diced

2 stalks celery, chopped

1-15 ounce / 425g can white shoe peg corn

10 ounces / 250g frozen butterbeans

1-16ounce / 453g diced tomatoes

2 potatoes, cubed

2-3 tablespoons apple cider vinegar

1 tablespoon brown sugar

⅓ cup / 75mil tomato ketchup

1 teaspoon Worcestershire sauce

½ teaspoon Tabasco sauce

3 tablespoons unsalted butter

A handful of fresh parsley

METHOD

Place chicken in a Dutch oven and add enough water to cover it. Add the onion, celery, salt and pepper. Boil until tender. Remove the chicken and tear it apart, removing all gristle and bones. Add the vegetables and then add the sauces and butter.
Skim off any fat.

Simmer on medium low heat for 2 hours. Once cooked, add the fresh parsley and a little more Tabasco sauce and serve!

See also Debbie's Southern Caviar, page 25 and Hoppin' John & Limpin' Susan, page 144

Alessio's Bucatini all' Amatriciana

This is a traditional and well-known dish from Amatrice, a small village in the Lazio region of Northern Italy. The recipe demands that guanciale (cured pork cheeks) be used. Nowadays, bacon is often used as a substitute, although guanciale has a much more interesting, less salty, delicate and exotic flavor. The following is basically the traditional recipe, with a couple of small additions. The use of onion and olive oil in Amatriciana is the source of many an argument, although I favor using them. I also like to add a couple of crushed juniper berries as a play on the cured guanciale.

— *Alessio Bax*

SERVES 4

INGREDIENTS

1 box of bucatini (I also like spaghetti). De Cecco pasta is my brand of choice for this recipe. Do not use fresh pasta for this.

5 slices of guanciale (cured pork cheeks) or five rashers thick sliced bacon, cut into cubes

½ large white onion

3 juniper berries, coarsely ground

4 tablespoons dry red wine

1 can / 500ml peeled tomatoes from San Marzano

1 can, or bottle / 500ml San Marzano Tomato Sauce

3 tablespoons Double Concentrate Tomato Paste

A pinch of sugar

Salt and pepper to taste

2 tablespoons extra virgin olive oil

A bowl of grated semi-aged pecorino cheese mixed with grated Parmigiano Reggiano

METHOD

Chop the onion very finely. Sauté it with the olive oil, tomato paste, sugar and guanciale or bacon until almost browned. Do not overdo this. The guanciale should become firm; its fat almost translucent, but do not caramelize the mix. Add the red wine and let sizzle. Add the peeled tomatoes and crush them with a spoon until they are unrecognizable as whole tomatoes! Then add the tomato sauce, lower the heat, add the ground juniper berries, salt and pepper to taste. Let it simmer for at least 30 minutes. When ready it will emanate a deeper smell than fresh tomato sauce, and the oils from the guanciale will have risen to the top. Stir the whole and let it simmer at very low heat until the pasta is ready.

To prepare the pasta bring a large pot of salted water to boil. Follow the instructions on the De Cecco box. The pasta must be firm to the bite (*al dente!*) and salted enough to be tasty when eaten alone.

When still slightly undercooked, use tongs to transfer the pasta into the saucepan. Let it finish cooking in the sauce and do not worry if some of the pasta water will end up in the sauce. Add the cheese mixture and keep stirring. Buon appetito!

Photo: Lisa-Marie Mazzucco

See also Sea Urchin Spaghetti, page 174 and Tiramisu, page 241

Pianist ALESSIO BAX creates a "ravishing listening experience" with his lyrical playing, insightful interpretations and dazzling facility. Having captured the coveted First Prize at the Leeds and Hamamatsu International Competitions and an Avery Fisher Grant, he has appeared with more than 100 orchestras under such greats as Sir Simon Rattle and Yuri Temirkanov, Vladimir Ashkenasy, Marin Alsop, Andrew Litton and many others. In the summer of 2015, he gave performances at fourteen major festivals on three continents.

As you can imagine, Alessio graduated with top honors at the record making age of 14 from the conservatory of his home town, Bari, Italy. He is now on the faculty at SMU in Dallas. We first worked together when he gave a superb solo recital in Hampton and as you will discover Alessio is a master chef as well as a master pianist!

www.alessiobax.com

Claire's Chicken with Pernod

Very simple but yummy. Love to you!

— Claire Bloom

SERVES 2

INGREDIENTS

2 boneless chicken breasts

1 onion, diced

2 cloves garlic, crushed

1 coffee cup Pernod

A generous handful fresh rosemary

Olive oil

METHOD

In a heavy black frying pan, pour enough olive oil to cover the base of the pan. Lightly fry the onion until it is soft, not brown. Add the garlic and let it melt with the onion.

Then add the chicken Cook on both sides until golden brown.

Add the pernod. Turn heat down to low.

Add the rosemary. Season with salt and pepper. Cover and cook for twenty minutes.

I don't quite know how CLAIRE BLOOM, CBE, obviously knew that I love the taste of Pernod...

It was Charlie Chaplin who first discovered the "beauty, talent and great emotional range" of the great British actress Claire Bloom when he invited her to co-star with him in the motion picture, *Limelight*. Subsquently Claire starred opposite such legends as Laurence Olivier (in many productions at the National Theatre and in the hugely popular PBS Series *Brideshead Revisited*). Other greats with whom she collaborated include: Richard Burton, John Gielgud, Paul Scofield, Ralph Richardson, Yul Brynner, George C. Scott, Paul Newman, and a host of others.

She played the role of Queen Mary in the highly acclaimed British motion picture, *The King's Speech*.

We had the pleasure of working together several times, and Claire graciously served as Mistress of Ceremonies at the Grand Opening and at the 5th Anniversary Gala at the American Theatre.

Claire receiving her CBE from HRH Prince William, The Duke of Cambridge, 2014.
Photo courtesy of Buckingham Palace

Claire Bloom at the opening of
The American Theater, 2000.
Photo: Gary Hess, Viewfinder Photographic Art

Michael and Claire, 1992
Photo: E. Holt Liskey

Olga Supphozova's Chicken & Potatoes

*This is a favorite of mine which I picked up from
the grandmother of an old boyfriend.*

— Olga Supphozova, aka Robert Carter

SERVES 4

INGREDIENTS

1 package of chicken parts (legs, thighs and wings)

1 large white onion

3 or 4 cloves chopped garlic

5 or 6 potatoes

Salt and pepper to taste

Herbs and spices of your choice — I prefer Italian spice seasoning

METHOD

Preheat the oven to 400F / 200C

Grease a large baking pan with a thin layer of olive oil. Place chicken parts, skin side up in the pan and season with the herbs and salt and pepper.

Dice the onion and finely chop the garlic cloves; spread liberally over the top of everything in the pan.

Cut the potatoes into uniformly sized pieces for even cooking and layer them over the top of the chicken. Season and drizzle with another light layer of olive oil.

Place the pan in the oven on the middle rack and bake for 35-40 minutes. The potatoes should be browned and tender when speared with a fork.

See also Bobby's Mac and Cheese recipe, page 146

OLGA SUPPHOZOVA made her first public appearance in a KGB lineup under dubious circumstances. After a seven-year-to-life hiatus, she returns to her adoring fans. When questioned about her forced sabbatical, Olga's only comment was "I did it for Art's sake!"

Art, however, had nothing to say.

ROBERT CARTER also known worldwide as OLGA SUPPHOZOVA and YURI SMIRNOV just recently signed on for his 21st season with Les Ballets Trockadero de Monte Carlo. Think about it.

Born and raised in Charleston, South Carolina (where else) he trained at the Ivey Ballet School and the Joffrey Ballet School. Before joining the Trocks, he was a member of the Florence Civic Ballet, the Dance Theatre of Harlem ensemble and the Bay Ballet Theatre.

www.trockadero.org

Vaughan Burdin Simpson
Helsinki Market
Watercolor

Vaughan's Louisiana Chicken Fricassee

*I love to serve this with a tossed green salad
and crusty French bread.*

— Vaughan Burdin Simpson

SERVES 4

INGREDIENTS

1 cut up chicken / 3 pounds / 1.5kg (or parts as preferred)

1 yellow onion, chopped

1 bell pepper, chopped

2 stalks celery, chopped

1 pound / 450g sliced mushrooms

½ cup / 125ml chicken broth

Flour

Vegetable oil

Rice (white rice is traditional, but I often use brown)

METHOD

Chop onion, bell pepper and celery.

Salt, pepper and flour the chicken. Brown it in vegetable oil.

Add chopped vegetables, mushrooms and cook until clear.

Add chicken broth or ½ cup water (or alternatively, ½ cup white wine).

Cover and cook at low heat for about 1 hour or until chicken is done and tender.

Serve over rice. Add more water to increase the gravy if needed and cook down for about two minutes.

See also Vaughan's recipes for Grits Soufflé, page 78 and Southern Spoon Bread, page 45

Flexibility and ingenuity are among the traits which encouraged the survival of Cajun culture and led to the creation of an exceptional cuisine. Cajun cooking reflects Cajun adaptability, concern with sensory pleasure and let's take life as it comes attitude.

From Vaughan's foreword to the immensely popular book, Talk About Good II

Chris' Chicken Marbella

My wife makes this recipe often for large family gatherings and it's always a big hit. This recipe is still good whether served hot, at room temperature or even cold, making it a good choice for large parties and buffet dinners. Enjoy!

— Chris Brubeck

SERVES 6 -8

INGREDIENTS

2 teaspoons minced garlic

1 teaspoon dried oregano

Salt & pepper

¼ cup / 60ml red wine vinegar

¼ cup / 60ml olive oil

½ cup / 64g pitted prunes

½ cup / 64g pitted green olives, cut in half

¼ cup / 60ml capers

5 pounds / 2.25kg chicken pieces (my wife prefers thighs for this recipe)

¼ cup / 4 tablespoons brown sugar

½ cup / 125ml white wine

2 tablespoons fresh parsley

METHOD

In a large bowl, mix first 8 ingredients. Add chicken, and coat completely. Cover and let marinate in refrigerator overnight. My wife has often added dried apricots to this recipe. She puts chicken, fruits, capers and marinade in plastic bags in refrigerator.

Layer chicken in single layer on shallow baking sheet, surround with prunes, capers, etc. Sprinkle chicken with brown sugar, and pour wine around chicken.

Bake for 1 hour at 350F / 180C. (Chicken is done when poked with a knife at the thickest point, all juices run clear.)

With slotted spoon, put the chicken, prunes, capers on a serving platter. Pour some of the juices on chicken and sprinkle with parsley. You can serve remaining juices in a gravy boat.

A master of bass trombone, piano, guitar and vocals, CHRIS BRUBECK first distinguished himself recording and performing with his father, the legendary Dave Brubeck. Now, he enjoys international acclaim as a performer, composer and band leader. His irrepressible on stage presence is matched by his fluid command of jazz blues, folk, funk, pop and classical genres. www.chrisbrubeck.com

Lemon Chicken with Capers & Hearts of Palm

This has always been one of my favorite recipes. Easy to make and really tasty! I love nothing more than entertaining family and friends. Enjoy.

— Toni Rizzo

SERVES 2

INGREDIENTS

2-6 ounce / 150g skinless, boneless chicken breast

2 tablespoons olive oil

1 garlic clove, crushed

3 button mushrooms, sliced

1 shallot, finely chopped

¾ cup / 175ml chicken stock

2 teaspoons corn starch

1½ tablespoons lemon juice

1¼ teaspoon lemon zest

2½ tablespoons capers

2½ Kalamata olives, halved

4 halves sundried tomatoes sliced

2-3 hearts of palm, sliced

1 tablespoon unsalted butter

2 tablespoons parsley, chopped

salt and pepper to taste

METHOD

Rinse the chicken breasts and pat dry. Place each between 2 sheets of plastic wrap and pound to ½" thickness. Season with salt and pepper. Heat olive oil in 10" skillet over medium high heat. Add crushed garlic clove and cook for about 1 minute. Remove and discard clove. Add chicken and cook for about 3-5 minutes per side until golden brown and cooked through. Remove chicken and loosely cover with foil. Add shallot and mushrooms to skillet and cook until slightly softened. Dissolve corn starch in chicken stock and add to skillet, along with lemon juice and zest. Increase heat and stir sauce until it begins to thicken (about 3 minutes). Decrease heat to medium and add capers, olives, sundried tomatoes, hearts of palm and half of the parsley.

Cook for about 3-4 minutes. Swirl the butter into the sauce. Add chicken to skillet and sprinkle with remaining parsley. Serve with sauce over cooked pasta of choice.

Toni, right, with Els Vuijsters at Bon Appétit, Lafayette.
Photo: Philip Gould

A native of Alexandria, Louisiana, TONI has always been passionate about cooking and celebrations. She moved to Cajun country in the late 1970's and joined the crew of Michael's Catering. She then went into business with Els Vuijsters and together they ran the long before its time Bon Appétit catering company where they made oven-ready, homemade meals, which were out of this world. Since then, she has continued to be a business owner and has served on numerous boards and committees, always finding herself working on stellar events.

Natalie's Favorite Chicken Pot Pie

You can bake the chicken ahead but I like to par boil the chicken pieces and use its water for the broth by adding two chicken sachets. You can also substitute the puff pastry for regular pastry dough. My kids love this.

— Natalie MacMaster

SERVES 4-6

INGREDIENTS

1 small onion, chopped

½ cup / 64g sliced mushrooms

2 carrots, chopped

2 stalks celery chopped

2-4 potatoes, cubed

METHOD

Preheat the oven to 400F / 200C

Sauté all of the above in 3 Tablespoons butter and a little oil until tender and crisp (about 10-12 minutes).

In a separate skillet add the following:

½ cup / 115g butter

½ cup / 64g flour

1 teaspoon salt

Pepper to taste

Melt the butter over medium heat. Blend in flour, salt and pepper and add — 3 cups / 700ml chicken broth — cook until thickened, stirring with a whisk to make sure it is nice and smooth — then add 3 cups / 380g cubed chicken and the vegetables.

Mix well and place in a greased casserole dish. Roll out thawed frozen puff pastry and cover the casserole. Make small slashes in the pastry and bake at 400F / 200C for 30 to 40 minutes or till golden brown and bubbly.

Cape Breton master fiddler, NATALIE MacMASTER was catapulted to international stardom when she released her first album, *Four on the Floor*, at the age of 16. She has now completed 11 albums and she continues to perform thousands of shows and to collaborate with a multitude of world renowned artists. Her music is filled with an invigorating mixture of toe-tapping jigs, reels and strathspeys (a Scottish dance in 4/4 time). Since she married fellow fiddler Donnell Leahy in 2002, her family and work life have been intertwined and they now have 5 beautiful children. Giving more than 100 concerts annually, her wonderful stage presence, intricate technique, elegance with the bow and her dedication to the age old Cape Breton traditions continue to amaze legions of fans. She has won countless awards and prizes and her recording with the legendary YoYo Ma won a coveted Grammy.

Natalie first came to the American Theatre with Leahy and subsequently returned in her *Christmas in Cape Breton* and her *Masters of the Fiddle* shows.

www.nataliemacmaster.com

Maria's Chicken Rouler

The American Theatre holds many happy memories for me. Working with Michael Curry was a life-changing experience. I met many remarkable people, including some of the artists featured in this book. It was a privilege to run the box office there for over a decade. I even got married on the stage! All of my guests were delighted as everyone got a great seat! Michael became like family to me and I'm grateful to still call him my dear friend.

— Maria H. Thomas

SERVES 4-6

INGREDIENTS

6 boneless, skinless chicken breasts

Spinach, steamed fresh (1 pound 450g) or 10 ounce / 250g frozen cooked & drained

1 clove garlic, minced

Olive oil

Goat cheese

Roasted red peppers

Salt & pepper

METHOD

Preheat oven to 400F / 200C

In a bowl, mix the minced garlic with the cooked spinach. Add salt & pepper to taste (you can also add a little bit of basil and oregano if you wish).

Clean your chicken well, then pound out the breasts so they are as flat as possible. Spoon your spinach mixture down the center of each breast, then top with your red peppers and a smear of goat cheese. Roll up your chicken breasts from the short end, then secure them with toothpicks.

Place your chicken rolls on a baking sheet lined with aluminum foil (you can use grease or cooking spray on an unlined pan if you wish).

Top each breast with a small amount of olive oil (maybe a teaspoon per breast) and a small amount of salt and pepper to taste. You can also add a splash of lemon juice if you have any handy.

Bake in the oven for 25 minutes and serve promptly.

SPECIAL INSTRUCTIONS

If you or any of your guests do not like goat cheese, this recipe is highly versatile. I've tried it using just cooked broccoli and cheddar cheese seasoned with salt and pepper instead of the goat cheese, spinach, and red peppers. You can also substitute feta cheese for the goat cheese. The possibilities are endless, just use your favorite cheeses and veggies.

Maria H. Thomas, a native of Hampton, won the Provost Scholarship and earned her BFA in Communications, Arts and Design from Virginia Commonwealth University. She served as a Gallery Assistant at the Charles H. Taylor Arts Center and then as House Manager and Box Office Manager at the American Theatre. Her passions and interests include movies, music, fashion, literature and Japanese culture and she started her own line of handmade, one of a kind knitwear items called *Go Go Milk*. She is the leader of the award-winning band, The Framers.

Dolores' Cajun Rice Dressing
Chicken Livers with Rice

*This recipe was always a favorite at pot luck
gatherings way back in the 1970's.*

— *Dolores Schuyler*

SERVES 4

INGREDIENTS

8 ounces / 200g chicken livers

Olive oil

½ cup / 125ml brown roux / gravy

1 pint / 500ml distilled water

1 large onion, chopped

2 cloves garlic, chopped

2 tablespoons green bell pepper, chopped

Salt, black and red pepper to taste.

METHOD

Chop the chicken livers into cubes and coat with flour.

Put olive oil into a black skillet, warm and add the livers.

Sauté for about 5 minutes

Add the onion, garlic and pepper.

Cook for another 5 minutes, stirring often.

Add the water and the gravy and bring to a boil.

Simmer on low heat for 30-45 minutes.

Serve over cooked rice.

DOLORES, or Sally as we all knew her, was a first rate cook and always had something going on the stove when you visited her on St. John Street. Active in the civil rights movement in the 1960s, she became Director of the Acadiana Sickle Cell Anemia Foundation, and we had adjoining offices in the First Presbyterian Church building. In addition to making great Cajun dishes, Sally had a wicked sense of humor.

Felicity's Cornish Pasties

Here is my take on Cornish Pasties.

— Felicity Ryan

SERVES 6

INGREDIENTS

Short crust pastry (or you can use readymade)

1.1 pounds / 500g strong bread flour

½ cup / 120g lard

½ cup / 120 g butter

1 teaspoon salt

¾ cup 175ml water

FILLING

1 pound / 450g good quality
beef skirt cut into cubes

1 pound / 450g potatoes, diced

½ pound / 225g rutabaga / swede, diced

2 or 3 onions, sliced

Salt and pepper to taste (2:1 ratio)

Felicity in her kitchen. *Photo: Jeremy Curry*

METHOD

Rub the fats together with the flour until the mixture looks like breadcrumbs.
Add water, knead pastry energetically. Leave to rest in fridge for 3 hours.

Roll out pastry onto a floured surface and cut into circles of about 20cm in diameter.
(A side plate is an ideal size!). Roll until it is about ¼" thick.

Layer the vegetables and meat on top of each circle, then season. Bring pastry around
and crimp edges. You can fold the pasty or bring the pastry up to the middle and crimp
across the top. The pasty needs to be sealed together. A local tip is to put a small knob of
butter on top of ingredients before putting pasty together.

Glaze the pasty with beaten egg or milk. Bake at 325F / 160C for 50-55 mins.

See also Felicity's recipes for Lemon Cheesecake, page 202, and Chocolate Cake, page 203

My sister, FELICITY RYAN, has been a professional cook and caterer all her life. After earning
her culinary degree from Brighton Technical College, she enjoyed a long and distinguished
career with the British Post Office, overseeing the menus and management of more than 100
restaurants and cafeterias. Before opening her own company, Felicity's Kitchen, she worked in
real estate.

Copper Country "Yooper" Pasties

Pronounced "Pass-tee", this is an Upper Peninsula variation on the traditional Cornish pasties from Great Britain.

— Ali Rogan

SERVES 4

INGREDIENTS

PASTIE CRUST

3 cups / 400g flour

1 cup / 250ml boiling water

1 teaspoon salt

1 cup / 250ml Crisco or lard

PASTIE FILLING

1 pound / 450g round, chuck beef or rump roast, cut into bite sized pieces

6-8 large potatoes, peeled and cubed

1 large yellow onion, chopped

1 Rutabaga, peeled and cubed (You can always substitute carrots)

¼–½ cup / 175g butter — depends on the amount of pasties

Salt & pepper to taste

Ali Rogan
Crystal Night
Installation at the Peninsula Fine Arts Center.
Photo: Rick Nelson

METHOD

In a large bowl add the boiled water to the Crisco/lard. Fold in the flour and salt. Refrigerate for at least one hour.

Divide this dough into 4-6 balls. Onto a floured surface, roll out the dough, smooth and easy, into 4-6" round circles about ¼" thick.

FOR THE FILLING

Combine all filling ingredients in a large bowl. Set aside the diced butter to add later.

Put 1½ cups / 200g filling on one half of the dough.

Place 1 tablespoon diced butter on top of the filling, then salt and pepper to taste.

Moisten the edges of the crust with water and fold the unfilled side over the filling to seal.

Pinch the edges and use a fork to crimp them down.

Place the pasties on a baking sheet lined with wax/parchment paper. Cut three or four slits into the top of the crust. Brush some milk on top of the crust, also.

Bake in a preheated oven at 350°F / 180C for one hour. Check at this point if the crust seems to be browning too quickly. If so, place aluminum foil on top of the pasties.

Remove from the oven. Serve with additional butter and ketchup, as desired.

Photo: Rick Nelson

Multi Award winning glass artist ALI ROGAN is the owner/partner of Cristallo Artisans in Newport News, Virginia. Having perfected her craft at such prestigious institutions as Penland, The Corning Glass Museum and Pilchuk Glass School she is a widely acclaimed member and leader of the contemporary art glass movement. Deeply dedicated to the further exploration of the art of glass, she leads workshops and classes throughout Southeastern Virginia. She is a Past President of the Peninsula Glass Guild and constantly teaches at the Governor's Magnet School for the Arts, at Tidewater Community College and other leading nonprofit art institutions.
www.alirogan.com

Paul's Imperial Deviled Crab

1st Sergeant Paul E. Bergh
Serial# 20360926

My father, Paul Bergh Sr., was a wonderful man who served his country in World War II and was shot in the head and laid on the field for six days before coming to. All of his men were dead and he managed to walk for hours and came in contact with a British Army unit. On his way, he came across a badly wounded solder still alive. He was too weak to carry the man. As best he could, he told the British unit approximately where the man was. Unfortunately my father worried about that man and died without knowing whether he was found alive. He could not talk because his skull went into his brain and he spent 9 months in the hospital in Italy. He had to learn to do many things over again. As most of the men from that generation, he did not talk about his experiences and only told me when I was 43.

This was his favorite recipe.

— *Pam Owen*

PAM OWEN spent 30 years in corporate America as internet manager for two different Fortune 500 companies. She now runs a successful healing practice.

INGREDIENTS

2 pounds / 900 g crab meat — remove pieces of shell

2 ounces / 50g butter

1 heaping tablespoon flour

Melt butter, stir in flour to thicken sauce.

Then add:

1 teaspoon salt

Several shakes of pepper

½ teaspoon Worcestershire sauce

½ teaspoon fresh lemon juice

1 teaspoon mustard

1 teaspoon hot sauce (Tabasco or Texas Pete)

Stir until mixed.

Add one cup milk.

With fork, mix sauce into crab meat, a little at a time until crab meat is completely moist. Place in shells.

Cover with a small amount of mayonnaise. Sprinkle with paprika.

Bake at 400F / 200C for 30 minutes or until top of crabs are browned.

Renee Olsovsky
Serving Bowl
Ceramics

David & Charlie's Thai Green Curry Crab Cakes

We are big believers in letting the taste, texture, and... je ne sais quoi... of a main ingredient shine through. For years we have been a proponents of crab cakes that taste almost solely of crab. Snce it's not an everyday meal but rather a celebratory splurge, why not go wild and let the crab shine!

While teaching a cooking class in Bronxville, New York, David was asked to develop some variations on the basic recipe. This got him thinking about various cultures that use crab and other shellfish in highly spiced dishes... and what ingredients might enhance, rather than overwhelm, the delicate sweetness of America's legendary "beautiful swimmers." He had an 'Aha! Moment' when he thought about a favorite Thai green curry that uses shrimp... The result made the crab purist in us very happy. We hope it will make you happy as well.

— David McCann & Charlie Hensley

MAKES 16 HORS D'OEUVRES OR 8 MAIN COURSE SIZED CAKES

INGREDIENTS

1 pound / 450g lump (not jumbo) fresh crab

1 stalk celery, diced very finely

1 scallion minced very finely (green and white parts)

1 large brown egg

1 tablespoon green curry paste

2 tablespoons mayonnaise

⅓ cup / 50g Panko breadcrumbs, plus more for dredging

⅓ cup / 50g finely shredded Thai (or regular) basil

Unsalted butter and oil for frying

METHOD

Thoroughly combine celery, scallion, egg, curry paste, mayonnaise, Panko, and basil. Add crab, and gently fold in.

Form gently into approximately 16 hors d'oeuvre-sized cakes, or eight larger, main course-sized cakes. Allow the cakes to rest in the fridge for about one hour. Just before cooking, dredge in more Panko.

For each four small, or two large, cakes, melt 1 tablespoon butter in 2 tablespoons oil on medium high heat. Gently fry cakes for approximately two minutes per side, until golden. As there is very little to bind them, these cakes are a bit fragile so handle with care and resist the urge to move them around in the pan a lot. A good non-stick skillet is your best friend here!

Serve simply… with a lime wedge, or some mayonnaise mixed with lime juice and more shredded basil.

NOTES: If you have a garden or a sunny windowsill… try growing some Thai basil. It's delicious and different enough that the flavor really jumps out at you... but regular Genovese is just fine. In a pinch, I've even used a bit of pesto!

You can even turn these into tiny cocktail party-sized cakes, but your guests may never want to leave!

Also feel free to add a shot of Tabasco or Sriracha if you'd like a little more heat.

DAVID MCCANN has appeared in theatres across the U.S., Canada and the U.K., including the Royal Shakespeare Company at the Barbican and on tour, Old Globe, Shakespeare Theatre, Pioneer, New World Stages, Kansas City Rep, St. Louis Rep, Denver Center, Alliance, Walnut Street, Syracuse, Delaware, Vermont Stage, Virginia Stage, Dorset, Olney, Wilma, Triad, Great Lakes/Idaho/Alabama/Orlando/Nebraska/Vermont Shakespeare Festivals, Meadowbrook, EST, Walkerspace, Ensemble (CA), and CT Rep. TV includes *Sex and the City, The Sopranos, ATWT, L&O,* and *L&O: CI.*

David is also a food writer, recipe developer, teacher, and playwright (*Great American Home Cooking, Every Day with Rachael Ray, A Christmas Carol (18 productions), Immortal Longings, Black & White, The Wake, Grand*). Follow his food blog at www.thisoldchef.com.

CHARLIE HENSLEY served as Artistic Director of the Virginia Stage Company for more than a decade and directed highly acclaimed productions of *Hamlet, Othello, The Glass Menagerie, A Perfect Ganesh* (among many others) and he starred in *The Mystery of Irma Vep.* He has always been committed to the development of new work and has received many prestigious awards and honors. His work has taken him to Japan, the Philippines, Korea and Austria and he is also acclaimed for his work with the Manhattan Class Company in New York.

www.charliehensley.com

Els' Confit of Duck or Duck Roast

*It is best to prepare this delightful dish at least
24 hours before you plan on serving it.*

— *Els Uitendaal Vuiysters*

INGREDIENTS

4 duck legs (about one pound each)

A handful of coarse sea salt, crushed

4 bay leaves, roughly torn and crumbled

4 cloves garlic, chopped

A generous handful of fresh thyme, torn and crumbled

3½ fluid ounces (100 ml) white wine

METHOD

Scatter half the salt, half the garlic and half the fresh herbs over the base of a shallow baking dish. Lay the duck, skin side up on top of this mixture and then scatter the remaining half of the salt, garlic and herbs on top.

Cover and refrigerate overnight. (This can actually be done two days ahead if you like).

Pour the white wine into a saucepan or large black pan that will accommodate the duck snugly.

Brush the salt off the duck and place the duck skin side down in the wine. Cover with a tight lid and heat at medium temperature until the wine starts to bubble. Turn the heat down and simmer for at least 4 hours, checking and basting occasionally. Once the duck is submerged in its own fat the legs should feel very tender when prodded.

Remove from heat and leave to cool. The duck can now be eaten.

TO ROAST A DUCK (if you cannot find duck legs)

Preheat the oven to 350F / 180c

1 whole duck, about 5 pounds

Prepare the whole duck as above, using the same ingredients.

Then place in the oven for at least 4 hours, checking and basting.

The duck can now be eaten OR IF YOU LIKE YOUR DUCK CRISPY (as I do) then follow the next step

Turn up the oven to 450F / 230C and bake for a further 30-40 minutes, turning and basting.

Serve with a homemade apple sauce, fried/boiled or roasted potatoes and a salad of, perhaps raw red cabbage.

Just pull the meat off the bone with two forks, as they do in the USA with pulled pork.

Et Voilà.

Photo: Philip Gould

Dutch born ELS VUIYSTERS is a fine cook. We first met when she and her family moved to Lafayette in 1975. She was a great Board member for The Fine Arts Foundation, a wonderful entertainer for guest artists and a fabulous planner of special events and galas. She worked almost three years for Michael's Catering and then she and her business partner Toni (see recipe on page 108) opened their own forward thinking business, Bon Appétit, in 1984. Els is now back in Holland and publishes an informative and humorous blog about cooking called *Dancing in my Kitchen*.

www.elsvuijsters.blogspotcom

Rob's Enchiladas Perfectos

Try these perfect enchiladas with your favorite beer.
Comer con placer y una cerveza de Guinness!

— Rob Faust

SERVES 4

INGREDIENTS

1-16 ounce / 400g can of Las Palmas Sauce — not Enchilada sauce

8 ounces / 240ml chicken broth

1 teaspoon Chilli powder

1 teaspoon onion power

1 teaspoon garlic powder

1 teaspoon cumin

½ teaspoon oregano

¼ teaspoon cinnamon

1 tablespoon fresh orange juice

1-8 ounce / 200g can of tomato sauce

1 package corn tortillas; plenty of grated Monterrey Jack cheese, black olives
(pitted and chopped) and a bunch or two of fresh green onions.

METHOD

Bring all of the above to a boil and simmer.

Preheat oven to 350F / 180C.

Dip corn tortillas in hot oil first for 2-3 seconds to soften. Then dip them through the
enchilada sauce. Stuff tortillas with the cheese, olives and onions.

Roll up and place in a greased baking pan. Cook for 12 minutes.

New Orleans native Rob Faust (Faustwork Mask and Mime Theatre) says:

> *"Kelli King is a great friend of mine whom I met at The Esalen Institute in Big Sur
> California. She is dancer, a dance professor at University of California Riverside,
> a food aficionado and home cooking goddess. She has a wicked good garden, loves
> to hike and surf, and uses power tools. What's not to love about Kelli?! You will agree
> even more after you try her perfect enchiladas with your favorite beer."*

Onward with appetite!

ROB FAUST is the Founding Artistic Director of Faustwork Mask Theatre. He designs and creates all of the masks used in the incredible Faustwork performances. Made from wood, leather, elastic, neoprene or Papier-Maché, his masks are primarily seen on stage but can also be occasionally seen in galleries because they are works of art. He has been commissioned to create works for such renowned companies as Momix, Pilobolus, The Paul Winter Consort and the American Conservatory Theatre.

Faustwork Mask Theatre continues to perform throughout the world at venues large and small. The company has been featured at the Metropolitan Museum of Art, the Sydney Opera House and Disney Hall and has enjoyed highly successful tours to Hawaii, Alaska, Canada, Italy, Germany, Hong Kong, Singapore, South Africa, Israel and Brunei.

Rob and I first met when I presented him in performance at Ogden Hall. He subsequently came to the American Theatre twice. I simply had to include his own thoughts about Mardi Gras and New Orleans — perfect:

"Growing up in New Orleans, celebrating Carnival every year has been a huge influence on my life as a mask maker and performing artist. Mardi Gras day is one enormous party that the entire city takes part in and to which the entire world is invited! It is an "in your face" participatory event and not merely a spectacle to watch. Every reveler is a walking show, provoking and reacting, doing short improvisations and moving on to the next encounter. Masks are great catalysts for the indulgences and jollity that the carnival inspires; people who might not ordinarily speak to one another, laugh, dance and misbehave together in the streets. After decades of celebrating the carnival season, I now find it very difficult to be shocked by public behavior anywhere in the world."

www.faustwork.com

Richard & Liz's Fish Curry

This curry works well with monk fish and is delicious with smoked haddock. Monk fish has a firm texture, which is good in curry, as does the chunkier end of a smoked haddock fillet.

— Liz Curry

SERVES 2 OR 3

INGREDIENTS

1 pound / 450g fish

Sunflower oil

2 garlic cloves, sliced and crushed

A piece of fresh ginger about 1 inch cube peeled and sliced (but you can add more according to your taste)

1 large onion, sliced

1 red pepper, deseeded and cut into strips

1 green Chilli, deseeded and chopped

1 heaping teaspoon of each of cumin, coriander, turmeric and cinnamon a little water

2 tablespoons (Blue Dragon or Thai Fish Sauce)

4 ounces / 115g cream cheese or similar (such as Philadelphia light)

Garnish with chopped mint or coriander

METHOD

Cut the fish into roughly one inch cubes. Fry these briefly in a little oil with the ginger and garlic. Remove from the pan with a slotted spoon and keep aside in a dish. Add the onion, pepper and Chilli to the pan, with a little more oil if necessary, to allow them to soften. This should take 2 or 3 minutes and shouldn't be overdone. Mix the dry spices with a little water and then add this mixture to the pan. Cook for a further 2 minutes. Remove the pan from the heat and return the fish, garlic and ginger to it. Add water to half cover the ingredients and add the fish sauce. Mix very gently avoiding breaking up the fish, bring up to the boil and simmer gently for 10 minutes. Taste, and season if necessary, and add the cream cheese. To do this add a little water to the cheese and stir well, then add to your pan. Bring up to the boil, reduce the heat and simmer gently. for 2 minutes.

Well, there you have it! It wasn't easy choosing the recipe as we like eating and like lots of foods but we do have this dish regularly and visitors always enjoy it.

This curry can be served with basmati rice or naan breads or you could try:

CAULIFLOWER RICE

(SERVES 3)

A small to medium cauliflower

2 tablespoons water

Chop the cauliflower into small pieces and pulse in a food processor, or similar, to the size of large breadcrumbs. Heat the water in a lidded pan then add the cauliflower. Season and steam over a moderate heat for 2 minutes.

Liz Curry
Playing in the fountains at Somerset House, August 2015
Photograph
That's me with my great niece Charlotte.

Both lifelong educators, my brother RICHARD and his wife LIZ are (like me) avid gardeners and therefore great experimental and improvisational cooks. Use what is on hand eh? As you can see from the photograph, Liz is an accomplished photographer and, in his retirement, Richard has been enjoying volunteering at the Citizens' Advice Bureau and doing some much appreciated research for me for this book!

Dame Cleo's Ace Fish Pie

— Dame Cleo Laine

SERVES 6

INGREDIENTS

2 pounds / 750mg potatoes, cubed

2 pounds / 750mg rutabaga / swede, cubed

3 ounces / 75mg butter

2 large brown eggs

1½ pounds / 750 mg filet of Smoked Haddock

2 bay leaves, crushed

6 peppercorns

¾ pint / 450ml milk

1 fresh leek, finely chopped

2 ounces / 50g plain flour

½ pint / 300ml white wine

3 large tomatoes, skinned and quartered

2 ounces / 50g cheddar cheese, grated

1 tablespoon sesame seeds

Salt and pepper to taste.

METHOD

Boil the potatoes and rutabaga together for 10-15 minutes until tender. Drain and add half of the butter and salt and pepper. Mash well and set aside.

Boil the eggs for 7 minutes. Shell and cool quickly under cold water. Cut the eggs into quarters and set aside.

Place the smoked haddock in a pan with the bay leaves, peppercorns and milk. Bring to a boil, cover and simmer for 12-15 minutes, until tender. Remove the fish from the pan, skin it and flake into large pieces and then set aside.

Strain the milk from the pan and set aside. Melt the remaining butter in a pan. Add the leek and fry for 5 minutes. Gradually stir and set aside. In the strained milk and white wine, cook until thickened, stirring constantly. Remove from the heat and gently add the fish, tomatoes, eggs and salt and pepper.

Transfer to a 4 pint (2.25litre) ovenproof dish and add the mashed potatoes and rutabaga.

Fork up the top of the pie and sprinkle with the cheese and sesame seeds.

Bake in a pre-heated 400F / 200C oven for 20-25 minutes until the crust is golden brown. Serve hot.

DAME CLEO LAINE is one of the legends that I grew up listening to. Her 1964 release with Sir John Dankworth, *Shakespeare and All That Jazz*, is still a bombshell. I remember telling myself way back then/when that we would work together. And we did — several times. What a pleasure.

Together with her husband/collaborator/band leader Sir John Dankworth, she established and maintains global acclaim not only as a first rate vocalist (with a phenomenal range) but also as a distinguished actress, teacher and festival director. She is the only female performer to have been nominated for Grammy Awards in each of the jazz, popular and classical genres.

The list of stars with whom Dame Cleo has collaborated would take another two pages!

In 1970, she and Sir John established the Stables Theatre in the grounds of their home. It was and continues to be a huge success, presenting 350 concerts and more than 200 educational and outreach programs a year.

www.stables.org

Anne's French Beef Stew

The monks love this. This recipe was given to me by the wife of one of my father's best friends. She was a fabulous cook. I have been making it for more than 30 years and everyone wants more!

— Anne Marie Shuyler

SERVES 6

INGREDIENTS

1 cup / 130g chopped onion

1 clove garlic, chopped

3 pounds / 1.3kg stew meat
(use very good beef)

½ cup / 125ml soy sauce

½ cup / 125ml red wine

2 tablespoons tomato ketchup

2 tablespoons red wine vinegar

½ teaspoon oregano

2 cups / 500ml water

2 cups rice

TOPPINGS

Sour cream

Chopped tomatoes

Chopped onions

Chopped red and yellow peppers

METHOD

Sauté onion and garlic. Add meat and brown. Add remaining ingredients and simmer for two hours. This can be done in the morning.

In the evening make the rice and reheat the stew. Serve over rice with chopped tomatoes, onions, peppers and sour cream on top.

Stew will be runny. Do not thicken it.

Needs only good bread and dessert for a great meal.

Use very good meat as this is what the meal is all about.

The Shuylers — Bill, Anne, Tia and Ada

Our entire family became fast friends with Michael when we first met at the opening ceremonies of Drepung Loseling Monastery's fantastic new prayer hall in Southern India. We have enjoyed re-connecting ever since and we are thrilled to be a part of this wonderful project… *Dining Among the Stars*.

Bill, the family and I first became involved with the monks when we hosted a group of 18 when they performed in the Smithsonian's Folk Life Festival which was attended by 1.5 million people. We have been happily hosting the monks on the Mystical Arts of Tibet tours ever since. The amazingly successful Smithsonian Festival was organized by the Conservancy for Tibetan Art and Culture, of which Bill is a Board member and currently serves as Secretary.

Anne uses her many talents helping non-profits; she is a member of the Smithsonian Women's Committee and arranges galas for organizations that serve abused children. Anne Marie loves to cook and entertains guests often but she is especially thrilled when the monks arrive and they can all enjoy this stew and some Traditional Mo-Mos as well as share those infectious and totally genuine smiles.

Mads' Danish Frikadeller

*Frikadeller is the traditional Danish dish that is very easy
to prepare. Basically, it is flat, pan-fried meatballs; great cold
the next day. Danes don't waste their food, so delicacies
from the night before are usually always served
on a sandwich the next day (or two)!*

— Mads Tolling

SERVES 4

INGREDIENTS

½ pound / 225g minced beef

½ pound / 225g minced pork

½ cup / 64g oatmeal
(bread crumbs another option)

1 cup / 130g flour

¼ teaspoon pepper

1 teaspoon salt

¼ teaspoon allspice, optional

1 to 1½ cups / 250-375ml milk

2 large brown eggs

1 minced or grated onion

2 tablespoons butter or margarine

METHOD

Mix the beef with the pork. Gradually stir in milk, onion and eggs. Add oatmeal or bread crumbs and flour to meat mixture and knead well. Add salt, pepper, allspice, if using, and about half the milk. Add eggs and onion and mix well. The Frikadeller gets better the more you mix it.

The mixture should be quite moist and soft, but not dripping. If too moist, add more flour and if too stiff, add milk. This makes it easier to form the shape of a meatball. Refrigerate mixture for at least 30 minutes or up to an hour.

When ready to cook, place a non-stick frying pan over medium-high heat, add a couple of tablespoons of margarine or butter and allow to melt. Shape Frikadeller by dipping a large tablespoon into melted margarine and using it to scoop a portion of mixture. A helpful trick is to smooth the mixture against the wall of the bowl.

Frikadeller should resemble a slightly flattened oval about the size of a small egg when placed in the pan. Fry in heated skillet. Don't crowd pan, Frikadeller should not touch while cooking. Fry 3-5 minutes on each side or until well-browned and no longer pink in center, then remove to a separate platter. Continuing shaping and frying, adding more butter as necessary.

If you have leftover Frikadeller, it is great to eat the next day. The Danish Frikadeller tastes great cold. A popular way to eat cold is on a Danish open-face sandwich, made on rugbrød (Danish rye bread) with red cabbage or pickle slices.

Two time Grammy Award winner, internationally known violinist and composer MADS TOLLING and his Quartet perform around the world. Having grown up in Copenhagen, Mads moved to the US at the age of 20 to pursue jazz studies. And that he certainly did (and continues to do so). He graduated cum laude from the Berklee College of Music and his career has been spiraling upwards ever since. He spent 9 years touring with Turtle Island Quartet and has had the pleasure of performing with such greats as Chick Corea, Ramsey Lewis, Kenny Barron and Paquito d'Rivera. In addition to leading his increasingly popular Quartet, Mads is a major composer; his specially commissioned Violin Concerto was given its world première to a capacity audience by the Oakland East Bay Symphony in 2015.

In his "spare" (does that exist) time, Mads enjoys tennis, golfing and hiking. He and his father climbed Mount Kilimanjaro together.

www.madstolling.com

Evelyn's Hamburger Steak

*This is oh so good and all my grandkids love it
served with mashed potatoes or rice.*

— Evelyn Childress McDonald

SERVES 4-6

INGREDIENTS

1 pound / 450g high quality ground beef

1 large brown egg

4 tablespoons breadcrumbs

Salt & pepper to taste

½ teaspoon onion powder

1 tablespoon Worcestershire sauce

1 tablespoon vegetable oil

1 cup / 130g thinly sliced yellow onion

2 tablespoons all-purpose flour

1 cup / 250ml beef broth

½ teaspoon coarse salt

METHOD

Get yourself a large bowl and in it mix the beef, egg, breadcrumbs, salt & pepper, onion powder and Worcestershire sauce. Form into 8 equal sized patties or burgers. Heat oil in a large black skillet over medium heat and fry the patties and onion until browned. Remove the patties and keep warm on a plate. Sprinkle the flour over the onions and drippings in the skillet getting all the bits off the bottom as you stir. Gradually mix in the beef broth and a little salt if desired. Simmer, stirring occasionally, over medium heat for about 5 minutes until the gravy thickens. Return the patties to the skillet, turn the heat to low and simmer gently for about 15 minutes.

EVELYN McDONALD was my right hand at Hampton Arts for 20 years. After a career at the Justice Department in Washington, D.C. and then in civil service at Fort Monroe, she joined the staff of Hampton Arts. She was a remarkable and generous soul who touched the lives of everyone with whom she came into contact. Her heart was full of pure love and there was no place for prejudice, jealousy or anger. She adored her family and showered love on her family which included 13 grandchildren and one great grandchild. Evelyn also worked tirelessly for many causes including her church and the Downtown Hampton Child Development Center.

Gary's Black Bean & Beef Chilli

This can also be a vegetarian meal, simply omit the beef!
I thoroughly enjoy combining my wonderful years as a chef with my ongoing
practice and studies in Eastern and Western nutritional therapy to promote the
use of foods and herbs as medicine in order to prevent and treat disease.

— *Gary Pecho*

SERVES 8

INGREDIENTS

1 Tablespoon olive oil

1 large sweet onion, diced (about 2 cups)

1 red bell pepper, diced (1 cup)

2 carrots, diced (½ cup)

2 teaspoons ground cumin

2 tablespoons chilli powder

½ teaspoon dried oregano

1 pound / 450g extra lean ground beef

1-28 ounce can / 794g can diced tomatoes

Salt and freshly ground pepper to taste

3-15 ounce / 425g cans black beans, drained and rinsed

1-16 ounce /454g refried black beans

METHOD

Heat the oil in a large stock pot or Dutch oven over moderate heat. Add the diced onion and gently fry until translucent. Add the carrots and the bell peppers and sauté for five minutes. Add the ground beef and raise the heat to high, browning the meat, breaking up the meat with the spoon until the meat is cooked through and is no longer pink. Add the ground cumin, oregano and chilli powder stirring until they are mixed in well. Reduce the temperature to low. Add the tomatoes, refried beans and black beans. Stir until well blended and simmer 30 minutes, stirring occasionally. Taste and correct seasoning before serving with salt and pepper.

Garnishing options: Avocado slices, diced onions, sour cream, cheddar flavored Goldfish or oyster crackers, shredded sharp cheddar cheese and a hot sauce of your choosing.

GARY PECHO, L.Ac., MSOM, is co-founder of Illinois Acupuncture Associates and Point of Health Acupuncture. He graduated cum laude from the Midwest College of Oriental Medicine and holds both a Master of Science and Bachelor of Science Degree in Nutrition. He earned a Culinary Arts Degree from the City and Guilds of London, then opened and successfully ran for several years a bed and breakfast/pub and restaurant in Jersey, the British Channel Islands.
www.mypointofhealth.com

Doucet's Jammin' Jambalaya

*All I can say is that you've never ever tasted
such a Jambalaya on the Bayou like this one.
Bon Appétit et laissez les bon temps rouler.*

— Michael Doucet

SERVES 6-8

INGREDIENTS

2 pounds / 1kg pork from your favorite butcher — or get a mini pork roast, plain, no stuffing from the supermarket

2 links good smoked sausage (andouille is always a good choice)

2 medium onions, chopped

1 large bell pepper, chopped

2 stalks celery, chopped

2 cloves garlic, chopped

1-8 ounce can / 200g Rotel diced tomatoes with green Chilli peppers

1-8 ounce can / 250ml chicken broth

1 tablespoon Kitchen Bouquet gravy

4 stalks green onions, chopped

2 cups brown / 250g rice

3 cups / 750ml water

Add some traditional Cajun seasonings such as Tony Chachere or Paul Prudhomme.

METHOD

Slice the pork into 1 inch cubes and season.

In a black iron pot heat up just a little oil over medium- high heat. Brown the pork until a slight gravy starts to form. Add the sliced sausage and brown some more. Mix in the vegetables along with the tomatoes, seasoning and then cook until wilted.

Add the chicken broth, Kitchen Bouquet, rice and water. Stir and mix well.

You should now have an inch to an inch-and-a-half of water above all of the ingredients.

Slowly lower a utensil into the water and when you touch something, measure from there.

Add water if needed.

Bring to a boil and then simmer until the water is just about out, stirring every now and then.

When you have about a quarter of an inch of water left on top, cover then reduce the heat to as low as it will go.

Simmer 10 minutes and remove the lid making sure that the water on the lid goes back into the pot.

Lift up the sides of the rice with a spatula and let the water run back to the bottom of the pot all around the sides. Do not stir at this point.

Cover and simmer for another 10 minutes.

Lift cover, stir in the green onions and Enjoy!

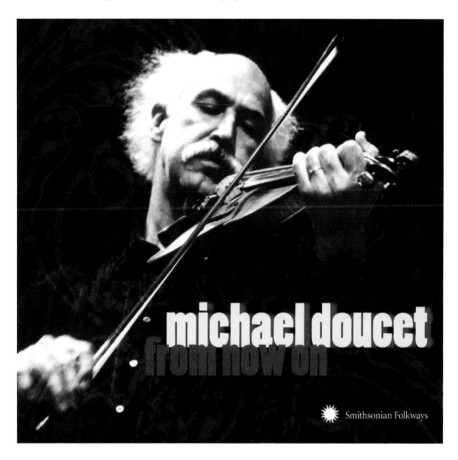

Fiddler extraordinaire, singer, songwriter, social historian and spiritual master, MICHAEL DOUCET is widely regarded as one of the pre-eminent musicians of our times. He founded "the best Cajun band in the land" (Beausoleil) in 1975 and continues to be globally rewarded, regarded and recognized for his leadership in bringing Cajun culture to a worldwide audience. He has won Grammy Awards, Fellowships from the National Endowment for the Arts and countless other accolades.

Having been "around" as they say, when I lived in Lafayette, Louisiana when Beausoleil was established and having followed the band enthusiastically ever since, Michael and I worked together on many occasions. He was one of our esteemed guest artists during the opening season of the American Theatre in 2000. Michael and Beausoleil subsequently played many more engagements at the Theatre and what joyous celebrations!

Merci beaucoup, Maestro!

www.beausoleilmusic.com

Bea's Luscious Leg of Lamb

I'd like to talk to you about lamb. Specifically leg of. You see, I like to give a lot of small dinner parties, and I find that leg of lamb is a wonderful thing to serve because, you know, you can prepare it well in advance.

You are interested aren't you?

Anyway, I start by removing all the fat and then I whip up this mayonnaise — mixture of olive oil, Dijon mustard, ground ginger, garlic and either rosemary or basil. I got the recipe from Julia Childs' Mastering the Art of French Cooking.

Then I smear the entire leg with this mayo mixture and let it sit for 3-4 hours. You can't over-marinate.

— Bea Arthur

SERVES: 4–6

INGREDIENTS

4lb freshly cut leg of lamb

A generous sprig of fresh rosemary leaves

4 or 5 cloves of garlic

4 tablespoons olive oil

2 teaspoons Dijon mustard

½ teaspoon ground ginger

Mint sauce (preferable) or mint jelly

METHOD

Preheat the oven to 350F / 180C

Bea liked to remove all of the fat from the lamb, but I actually prefer to leave some so that the "mayo like mixture" turns crispy.

Chop the garlic into small wedge-like pieces and insert into the lamb by cutting little pockets into the meat. This way the garlic infuses the meat from the inside out.

Mix the olive oil, mustard and ginger and smear over the entire joint.

Place in the oven and roast for at least an hour and a half. Baste as necessary.

Increase the oven temperature to 375 and bake for a further 10-15 minutes.

To make the complete dinner, Bea used to like to serve broiled tomatoes, roasted Japanese eggplant or potatoes.

I love to par-boil potatoes and parsnips and then add them both to the roasting dish at least an hour before the dish is due to be ready. And I have to add, there is nothing better than lamb leftovers… make sandwiches or shepherds' pie.

Serve with the mint sauce as a garnish.

Talk about a classic ice-breaker. This was the opening of BEA ARTHUR'S wonderful one woman show, *Bea Arthur on Broadway: Just Between Friends*, with Billy Goldenberg at the piano when our paths crossed in 2005. We spent a glorious three days together in Hampton, Virginia. Bea Arthur was a Tony Award and Emmy Award winning actress who stole the hearts of millions of fans. She is probably best loved for her iconic roles in *All in the Family*, *Maude* and *The Golden Girls*. But, her solo show was pure theatre. Naturally, I told her all about Ella Fitzgerald's gift to me of salad recipes and the lovely and gracious Bea told me, "Add my lamb recipe to your collection and feel free to adapt it in any way you like."

Renee's Lasagna for the Lamas

This was always a great favorite when the monks could have some much needed "downtime" and "playtime" as you can see from the photograph of them playing basketball (with no rules, of course) in my garden.

— Renee Olsovsky

VEGETARIAN LASAGNA WITH NO TOMATO SAUCE

SERVES 12

INGREDIENTS

FOR THE WHITE SAUCE

¼ cup / 50g melted butter

⅓ cup / 50g flour

1 teaspoon salt

3 cups / 750ml milk (may use low fat or skim)

12 lasagna noodles, cooked al dente

1 cup / 128g / 250g Mozzarella cheese (may use part skim milk)

FOR THE CHEESE FILLING

1-10 ounce / 250g package frozen spinach

2 cups / 500g Ricotta cheese, or whipped cottage cheese. I use Ricotta.

2 large brown eggs

¼ cup / 40g grated Parmesan cheese

1 teaspoon dried basil

½ teaspoon dried oregano

1½ teaspoons garlic powder

¼ teaspoon black pepper

FOR THE VEGETABLES

1-2 tablespoons light olive oil

8 ounces / 200g sliced or chopped mushrooms

2 cups / 250g grated carrots

½ cup / 64g chopped onions

1 cup / 125g finely chopped bell peppers

METHOD

Preheat oven to 350F / 180C

FOR THE WHITE SAUCE

Use a 1 quart saucepan to melt the butter over low heat.

Stir in the flour and salt.

Cook over a low heat, stirring constantly, until bubbly.

Remove from heat and stir in the milk.

Heat to boiling, boil and stir 1 minute, stirring constantly.

Cover and keep warm. If the sauce thickens, stir in a little milk until it reaches the desired consistency

FOR THE CHEESE FILLING

Combine spinach, ricotta cheese, eggs, Parmesan cheese, basil, oregano, garlic powder and pepper together in a bowl and set aside.

FOR THE VEGETABLES

Cook the carrots, add mushrooms, onions, and bell peppers in a frying pan in a little olive oil until soft and tender. Set aside.

TO ASSEMBLE LASAGNA

Place 4 noodles in the bottom of the pan.

Top with half of the cheese filling, ½ cup of the Mozzarella cheese and then 4 more noodles.

Spread cooked vegetables on top of the noodles. Then pour and spread half of the white sauce over top of the vegetables. Place the remaining noodles over that.

Then spread the remaining cheese mixture on top of the noodles. Pour and spread the remaining white sauce over that.

Sprinkle with the other ½ cup Mozzarella cheese.

Bake for 45 minutes. Let stand 10 minutes before serving.

RENEE, a practicing Buddhist and very creative potter loves to serve this dish to the monks when they are in town. A longtime volunteer at The American Theatre and The Charles H Taylor Arts Center, her work has been featured in many recent exhibitions in Southeastern Virginia. Renee is also deeply committed to various other causes including animal rights, and she is a regular volunteer at the Animal Aid Society.

Susan's Red & White Lasagna

I like to add Stouffer's Spinach Soufflé to my lasagna but it is optional. It does add taste and texture to the layers. Try it!

— Susan Stapleton McLaurin

SERVES 6

INGREDIENTS

RED SAUCE

1 onion

1 garlic clove

1-12 ounces / 340g can tomato paste

1-4.5 ounce / 396g can crushed tomatoes

1 bay leaf, crushed

½ cup / 125ml water

1 tablespoon fresh basil

1 teaspoon sugar

½ cup / 125ml red wine

1 tablespoon fresh parsley

WHITE SAUCE

4 tablespoons butter

½ / 64g flour

½ teaspoon nutmeg

Pinch of salt & pepper

2 cups / 250ml milk

METHOD

Add 1 packet Lasagna, mozzarella and parmesan cheese (grated) about ½ cup each. Add more to taste. Chop onion & garlic clove and cook in olive oil until translucent, add tomato paste and cook for 5 minutes over med-high heat. Add the crushed tomatoes, water, basil, bay leaf, sugar, wine and parsley and cook 30 minutes.

To make white sauce combine butter and flour in pot. Add nutmeg, salt & pepper. Slowly add milk over medium heat stirring constantly until thick. Cool.

Cook lasagna noodles.

LAYER AS FOLLOWS

Tomato base

Lasagna

Spinach, if using

White sauce (2 tablespoons)

Mozzarella cheese

Parmesan cheese

Susan Stapleton McLaurin
Supermoon Madness
Mixed Media
Photo: Pac McLaurin

SUSAN is a papermaker/mixed media artist whose work has been exhibited nationally and internationally. She maintains a studio in North Carolina, and incorporates all kinds of materials — pastel, pencils, markers and paint — and images from unusual sources to her work. Susan lived in Virginia for many years where she was part owner of a gallery in Richmond's historic Fan District. She has staged multiple solo and joint exhibitions in Washington D.C., San Miguel de Allende in Mexico, UVA in Charlottesville and in Chapel Hill and Raleigh, North Carolina.

www.susanmclaurin.com

Low Country Hoppin' John
& Limpin' Susan

*Well, I usually just have the Hoppin' John for New Year's Day
but sometimes like to incorporate the Limpin' Susan so they'll be
together to start a New Year! This is delicious and easy.
Low country* cookin'. My aunt and grandmother
served rice and some type of peas at every dinner.*

— Debbie Brooks

SERVES 4

SO HERE WE GO…HOLD ON. FOR THE HOPPIN' JOHN

INGREDIENTS

1 large onion, chopped

2 cloves garlic, minced

2 tablespoons butter

2-16 ounce / 425g cans black eye peas,
drained and rinsed

1 cup / 128g uncooked rice

Salt and pepper to taste

A generous pinch or two of crushed red pepper

FOR THE LIMPIN' SUSAN

3-4 slices / rashers bacon

1 pint / 250g okra

1 cube chicken bouillon

METHOD

Sauté the onion and garlic in the butter in a large cast iron skillet. Add the remaining ingredients and bring to a boil. Reduce heat to a simmer for approximately 20 minutes until the rice is cooked.

Chop the bacon and fry until it is crisp. Drain onto paper towels. Barely cover the okra with water and a small amount of chicken broth in a saucepan and bring to a boil.

Gently simmer until it is almost done. Remove the okra and slice into pieces. Then put the sliced okra into a skillet with bacon and cook for a further 2-3 minutes.

This can be then added to the Hoppin' John to make the meal complete.

*See also Debbie's Brunswick Stew, page 97 and
Southern Caviar, page 25*

*Low Country is the coastal area of South Carolina from Pawley's Island to the Georgia state line. There is an abundance of seafood in the area that is influenced by African and Caribbean cuisine, which are the hallmarks of this type of dish.

Anderson Johnson, *Cat with Angel, Oil on cardboard, Collection of the Author*

Herman's Mac & Cheese

This is one of my favorite comfort foods.
It goes well with filet mignon and petit pois!
— Herman Mhire

SERVES 8

INGREDIENTS

2 cups / 250g uncooked penne pasta

8 ounces / 225g sharp cheddar cheese grated

8 ounces / 225g Monterey Jack cheese grated

8 ounces / 225g parmesan cheese grated

2-12 ounces cans / 700ml evaporated milk

Dairy milk as needed

3 large brown eggs

Salt and pepper

8 teaspoons unsalted butter

Herman Mhire, *Vegetarian Mask*, Photograph

METHOD

Preheat oven to 350F / 180C

Boil pasta in salted water until cooked. Drain in a colander.

In a large mixing bowl, beat three eggs. Add the evaporated milk and parmesan cheese. Salt and pepper to taste. Whisk thoroughly.

Spray interior of casserole dish with non-stick spray.

Sprinkle the grated Monterey jack cheese across entire bottom of casserole dish. Distribute cooked pasta over jack cheese.

Pour egg, parmesan cheese and evaporated milk mixture over pasta. Add enough dairy milk to cover pasta.

Distribute grated cheddar cheese and butter over pasta.

Bake for 30 to 40 minutes until cheddar cheese begins to brown.

Remove from oven and allow casserole to set for a minimum of 30 minutes before serving.

A native of Lafayette, HERMAN was named Distinguished Professor of Visual Arts at the University of Louisiana. As Director of the Paul and Lulu Hilliard University Art Museum, he organized more than 200 major exhibitions. Trained as a painter and printmaker, Herman shifted to photography after his retirement and his recent works have been shown at the Acadiana Center for the Arts, the Contemporary Arts Center in New Orleans and the Sara Nightingale Gallery in New York. His latest series entitled Shells includes a diverse collection of images — both real and imagined — from nature. www.hermanmhire.com

Yuri's Mac & Cheese

This is a twist on my Mother's recipe and it is always a hit!
Sometimes, the measurements are kind of vague
but I usually always just eyeball it.

— Olga Suppozhova / Yuri Smirnov / Bobby Carter

SERVES 4

INGREDIENTS

1 pound / 450g elbow macaroni or ziti pasta

1 pound / 450g grated cheddar cheese (I like to use a mix of cheddar and mozzarella)

1 stick / 113g butter

1 tablespoon yellow mustard

3 large brown eggs

1-1½ 12 ounce cans / 500ml evaporated milk

4 slices/rashers crisp fried bacon, drained and crushed.
(You can substitute turkey bacon if you like.)

Plain bread crumbs

Salt and pepper to taste

METHOD

Fry the bacon until crisp. Drain onto paper towels to remove the grease.

Boil the pasta until it is fully cooked and drain well. Pour the hot drained pasta into a large mixing bowl and immediately add the butter and stir until fully melted.

Add the cheese and continue stirring until the cheese is evenly distributed throughout. Add your mustard and bacon, stir and add the salt and pepper.

Add your eggs and stir until everything is evenly mixed.

In a medium dish or baking pan, pour the mixture and spread evenly with a spoon or spatula.

Pour the evaporated milk until it is just level with the top of the mixture. Spread a layer of breadcrumbs over the top and place in the oven at 375F / 190C for 40 minutes or until the crust is browned lightly.

Remove from the oven and let set for about 15 minutes to allow the hot mixture to firm before serving.

See also Chicken & Potatoes, page 102

At the age of sixteen, YURI SMIRNOV
ran away from home and joined the Kirov
Opera because he thought Borodin was
a prescription barbiturate. Luckily for Les
Ballets Trockadero de Monte Carlo, he soon
discovered that he did not know his arias
from his elbow and decided to become a
ballet star instead.

www.trockadero.org

Wartime Deviled Mackerel

I found this wonderful recipe in my foster grandmother's recipe book… this was published by the BBC in a small "wartime" recipe booklet in the early 1940's when rationing was in full force.

— Michael Curry

SERVES 4

INGREDIENTS

4 medium sized mackerel

1 tablespoon Colman's Mustard mixed with a little vinegar

2 tablespoons butter

1 tablespoon sugar (if you can get it)

1 bay leaf, crushed and torn

1 spring onion, chopped

METHOD

Filet the mackerel and remove the back bones. Wash well.

Mix the mustard and sugar with half the butter.

Spread this paste on the insides of the fish and fold the fish bodies together again.

Melt the rest of the butter with the bay leaf and onion.

Grill the fish for 8-10 minutes, turning several times.

I love the fact that the recipe calls for sugar "if you can get it". Remember rationing was pretty harsh during the Second World War and indeed up until the early 1950's.

There is nothing better than fresh mackerel… go find a fishmonger and get some. The best I think I ever had was at a waterside restaurant in Istanbul.

Photo: Alexander Kravets

Chef Bobby's Meatloaf

— Bobby Huber

SERVES 4-6

INGREDIENTS

3 pounds / 1.5kg ground beef

¼ pound / 125g smoked Surry sausage (if you cannot find Surry sausage, try andouille)

1 large yellow onion, chopped

¼ cup / 30g diced green pepper

¼ cup / 30g diced celery

3-4 cloves garlic

1 cup/ tomatoes and juice

1 tablespoon Worcestershire sauce

1 teaspoon Sriracha

2 teaspoons / cubes beef consommé

¼ teaspoon Cayenne pepper

¼ teaspoon white pepper

¼ teaspoon black pepper

1 teaspoon cinnamon

3 large brown eggs

1 cup / 125g bread crumbs

4 or 5 slices / rashers bacon for wrapping — applewood smoked bacon was always Bobby's choice

Photo courtesy of The Virginian Pilot/ John H. Sheally, II

METHOD

Preheat oven to 300F / 150C

In a food processor, purée everything except the ground beef, bread crumbs, and bacon. Blend the ground beef into the mixture, then add the bread crumbs and wrap with bacon, holding it together with a toothpick or two if necessary.

Place in a loaf pan.

Bake for 40 minutes. Serve over mashed potatoes, and top with barbeque sauce and frazzled onions if desired.

Chef BOBBY HUBER was an incredible host, generous spirit and all around great cook. He passed away way before his time in 2014. His wife Heidi sent this recipe and I am so happy to include it while honoring the great memories we had at Fire and Ice and at Bobby's Americana in Hampton as well as at Bobbywood in Norfolk. We enjoyed many a great evening together before and after performances and his food and presentations were exceptional.

Traditional Tibetan Mo Mos
Meat or Vegetarian Steamed Dumplings

The more you knead, the better the dough. . .

— The International Campaign for Tibet

MEAT MO MOS
SERVES 4-6

INGREDIENTS

1 pound / 4 cups / 450g flour

1 to 1½ cups / 300 ml distilled water

1 pound / 450g choice ground beef

2-3 stalks celery, chopped

1 small onion, chopped

2 green / spring onions chopped

A generous handful of fresh cilantro

1 tablespoon vegetable oil

2 tablespoons soy sauce

Salt and pepper to taste.

METHOD

In a large bowl, place the flour and make a well in the center. Slowly add water, using just enough for the dough to hold its consistency. Knead the dough until it is firm but supple.

Divide the dough into four parts. Roll each one out with a floured rolling pin and then, using a 3" cookie cutter (or upturned glass) cut out the momo 'skins' or covers.

To each of the momo skins add 1 Tablespoon of the mixture and then pinch the dough together from side to side. Crimp with a fork.

Place the ground beef, chopped onion, cilantro and celery into a large bowl and mix thoroughly.

Heat 2 Tablespoons oil in a black skillet and add the dumplings one by one, letting their bottoms brown.

Add the water and quickly cover the pan. Bring to a boil. Once the pan starts steaming and the water evaporates, the mo-mos are ready.

Adding a little water to the celery and the greens and herbs mixture will help to keep the mo-mos juicy and succulent.

Try these with Tibetan Martza (Chilli Sauce, page 73)

Mo Mos with Martza
Photo: Dianne Hoffman

VEGETARIAN MO MOS

SERVES 4

INSTEAD OF THE GROUND BEEF FILLING, YOU CAN USE A TOFU AND GREEN BEAN,
MUSHROOM AND CHEESE OR POTATO AND CABBAGE FILLING. ALL EQUALLY AS GOOD.

INGREDIENTS

5 or 6 medium sized potatoes

1 medium onion, chopped

½ cup / 64g fresh chopped cilantro

½ cup / 64g fresh chopped scallions

¼ cup / 50g frozen sweet peas

4 tablespoons unsalted butter

1 teaspoon salt

METHOD

Boil the potatoes until soft — about 20 minutes. In a separate pan sauté the onion,
cilantro peas and butter. Mash the potatoes and add the sautéed mixture. Follow the
directions for the meat Mo Mos.

Allow to cool for a few minutes before serving.

See also Tibetan Flat Bread, page 42

www.savetibet.org

Ashraf's Moussaka

A great trick my Mother taught me to make delicious Moussaka is to prepare the eggplant by slicing it, sprinkle with salt and place in a colander over a bowl for at least two hours. This drains the acid away and makes the eggplant much tastier. Also, by adding the apple vinegar, the dish is complete! In Egypt, we often eat this dish, even cold for breakfast! Try it. It's very good, trust me.

— Ashraf Omran

SERVES 4-6

INGREDIENTS

1 large black eggplant/aubergine

1 green pepper

1 red pepper

1 yellow pepper

1 orange pepper

3 large tomatoes

1 large yellow onion

4 medium-large potatoes

6 cloves garlic, sliced

1-10 ounce / 250g can tomato sauce

A pinch or two of coarse salt

2 tablespoons cumin

1 tablespoon red pepper

2 tablespoons apple cider vinegar

Vegetable oil

METHOD

Preheat the oven to 400F/200C

Heat the tomato sauce and one fresh tomato in a saucepan. Add the cumin and red pepper and vinegar. Slice the potatoes, onions and other two tomatoes. In a deep frying pan, fry the potatoes first; remove and drain. Fry the eggplant until golden brown then remove and drain. Finally, fry all of the peppers for just one or two minutes. Put a little oil, enough to coat, in a large Pyrex dish. Layer the onion, peppers and potatoes, and then the eggplant and one more layer of potatoes. Finally add another layer of peppers and tomatoes.

Bake for 30-40 minutes.

ASHRAF OMRAN earned his PhD from Old Dominion University in 2010 and is now a Control Engineer at Case New Holland Industrial (a division of FIAT International) in Burr Ridge, Illinois. He earned his Bachelor and Master Degrees from Cairo University and has been published in almost four dozen highly prestigious journals and magazines. He has presented seminars and lectures at international conferences in Istanbul, San Francisco and Salt Lake City and has recently submitted no fewer than 8 patent applications… seven of which have already been approved!

Graham & Barbara's Mushroom Supreeze

Barbara is standing beside me now dictating instructions.
This is an easy and light lunch.

— *Graham Garton & Barbara Howson*

SERVES 2

INGREDIENTS

2 large mushrooms, peeled

2 fish cakes

2 tomatoes, grilled or 1½ ounce / 300g can baby broad beans

Fresh basil, salt and pepper to taste

METHOD

Skin the mushrooms and pop into frying pan with light oil, pepper, put a blob of oil in each mushroom to keep moist. Remove and set aside. Fry the fish cakes in light oil, or cook in oven on baking sheet, with basil. When both are cooked, pop fish cakes on top of mushrooms, serve with baby broad beans or peas and/or grilled tomatoes.

BOTH GRAHAM AND BARBARA were huge influences on my life in boarding school. Graham was Director of Music and his wife Barbara was a leading soprano, often appearing as soloist with the school orchestra (in which I played Principal Bass). In addition to being a fine organist, pianist, conductor and composer Graham was a fantastic teacher. He taught me and generations of other lads the joys of music of all kinds — most especially Handel's Oratorios and works by Benjamin Britten, Edward Elgar and others which we performed both at school and in the Watford Town Hall. Graham also coached me (very successfully, I must add) in my Associated Boards exams in Piano, Theory of Music and Double Bass.

Frank's Penne Pasta

This is a good dish for vegetarians but meat eaters feel free to add your own pre-cooked homemade meatballs or cooked lamb riblets into the sauce when it is first simmering.

This sauce was an oft-served favorite in my Grandma Sophie's home. Holidays, birthdays, well..most days. She cooked up until her passing at 93. When she left I missed her terribly and the scent of her sauce...but I got the simple recipe and I share with you. In the day, the sauce was made by scratch but she used Hunt's as the base for the last decades and it works. I've tossed in a few of my own touches but the essence remains. The celery stick is key for flavor. And lots of garlic never hurts. Enjoy! Mangia!

— Frank Ferrante

SERVES 6-12

INGREDIENTS

3-6 ounce / 1790g cans Hunt's Tomato Sauce

1 whole yellow onion

1 head of garlic (two heads if you are feeling nutty)

Olive oil

1 cup / 128g Parmesan cheese

Cracked black pepper

1 large stalk of celery

1 cup / 250ml red wine

3 basil leaves

METHOD

Empty three cans of Hunt's Tomato Sauce into a large sauce pan. Rinse each can with about 1 inch of water and add to the sauce. Cook on high and when sauce begins to boil turn down to low heat. While that simmers, chop the onion and garlic. Sauté (liberally coat the pan) with olive oil in a frying pan or skillet until golden. Add the sautéed onions and garlic into the sauce. Add the celery, basil leaves, and a cup of parmesan cheese, cracked black pepper to taste and three quarters cup of red wine. Stir ingredients. Leave lid on but allow steam to escape. Let simmer on low for 2½ hours. Check and stir occasionally so ingredients do not stick to bottom of the pan.

Photo: Frank Ferrante Productions

Any pasta will do but my preference is penne. Cook the pasta in boiling water with two table spoons of salt. When the pasta is al dente...firm to the bite...it is done. Strain the pasta but do not rinse.

Place half of the pasta in a large bowl and ladle sauce upon it. Add the rest of the pasta and ladle again. Keep extra sauce in a side bowl. Serve.

My Grandma Sophie would often add thin cooked, steamed green beans to the pasta sauce and it was a nice touch.

I happen to like black cracked pepper on my pasta as did my Grandpa Tony.

Hailed by *The New York Times* as "the greatest living interpreter of Groucho Marx' material, FRANK FERRANTE is an actor, director and producer. Discovered by Groucho's son Arthur, Frank created the title role in *Groucho: A Life in Revue* (written by Arthur) off Broadway in which he portrayed the legend from the age of 15 to 85! Frank earned the New York Theatre World Award for this performance as well as an Outer Critics Circle Nomination. He reprised the role in London's West End and was nominated for the Laurence Olivier Award for Comedy Performance of the Year.

He has performed the role more than 2500 times in more than 400 cities (including twice in Hampton). He recently toured the show in Australia for 4 weeks to great critical acclaim.

Frank has also taken leading roles in many regional theatres and directed the world première of the Pulitzer finalist *Old Wicked Songs*. He also directed *MASH* star Jamie Farr in *George Washington Slept Here*.

www.eveningwithgroucho.com

Mark's Pasta Puttanesca

Pasta Puttanesca is a wonderful, earthy tasting pasta sauce that features anchovies, capers and olives to give it a strong, salty flavor.

— Mark Summer

SERVES 4

INGREDIENTS

2 tablespoons extra virgin olive oil.

¼ teaspoon crushed red pepper (optional)

2-6 cloves fresh garlic, depending on taste.

4-5 anchovies / 2 ounces / 50g

½ diced yellow onion

1 teaspoon capers

¼ cup / 64g chopped pitted black olives

1-28 ounce / 794g can Italian plum tomatoes, crushed or whole.

Oregano, fresh ground black pepper to taste, chopped fresh basil to taste.

1 pound / 450g dried pasta

METHOD

Begin with the olive oil in a large skillet. Turn the heat on low and while warming the oil, add the red pepper flakes, amount depending on your preference — this can be omitted if you desire a milder sauce.

Mince the garlic and sauté in the oil, taking care not to burn the garlic. Add chopped yellow onion. When the onion is translucent, add the anchovies, amount depending on how strong a flavor you desire. Cook the anchovies until they melt into the onions and garlic.

Add the can of plum tomatoes. They can be crushed or whole. If whole, use a potato masher to crush tomatoes in skillet. Simmer for a while, adding the capers. Add the olives. Add oregano and fresh ground pepper and chopped basil.

While sauce is simmering, boil salted water for pasta in large pot. If you are using brown rice pasta, allow some extra time for cooking. When pasta is *al dente*, flush with cold water and drain in colander.

Serve with a fresh basil leaf on the plate, and have plenty of freshly grated parmesan cheese on hand.

Bon Appetit!

Photo: Bill Reitzel

MARK SUMMER was the original/founding cellist in the fabulous Turtle Island Quartet and performed around the world with them from 1985 until 2015 when he left to pursue a solo career. Besides Turtle Island (which has now released 15 albums) Mark has performed with many other crossover artists including the Jazz Chamber Trio with Alon Yavnai and clarinetist Paquito d'Rivera. He has also composed pieces for solo cello and gave the world première of David Balakrishnan's *Force of Nature* with the Alexandria Symphony in 2011. Mark graduated from the Cleveland Institute of Music and, before joining Turtle Island, performed in the Winnipeg Symphony for three years.

www.marksummer.net

Quartetto's Sicilian Pasta

When you make this dish for your friends LIE!
Do not tell them that this dish has ANCHOVIES!

When anchovies are cooked they dissipate in the oil and
the saltiness diminishes so they will never know.

You are the chef and are smarter and wiser. Traditionally
this dish does not have white wine but I add it
because I like how it cuts the oil.

— Peter De Sotto

SERVES 4-6

INGREDIENTS

1 pound / 450g spaghetti

½ cup / 250ml olive oil

1 cup / 128g walnuts

1 cup / 128g raisins

1-2 ounce / 50g can anchovies, drained

10 finely sliced garlic cloves (more is always better)

1 cup / 250ml white wine

Parmigiano reggiano

Fresh chopped parsley

2 or 3 cayenne peppers

METHOD

Cook your pasta while preparing the sauce.

Sprinkle the cayenne peppers in oil and lightly brown. Browning the pepper reduces the burn and leaves a nice toasty flavor. Add the garlic and sauté over medium heat until soft, then add the walnuts and raisins.

Cook until the walnuts turn brown and the raisins get puffy, add your white wine to make the reduction.

Serve in a big colorful bowl and sprinkle with Parmigiano cheese and chopped parsley.

Serve with lots of wine and drink wine to excess! (Makes for a better party)

Buon Appetito!

Virtuosic showpieces, romantic tenor arias, pyrotechnical solos, blazing gypsy show pieces, multi-instrument mastery and a World Accordion Champion — this is Quartetto Gelato.

For 25 years, this dazzling ensemble has enchanted audiences and critics worldwide with their exotic blend of musical virtuosity, artistic passion and humor. Classical in training, eclectic by design Quartetto Gelato also offers the bonus of a brilliant operatic tenor. With a repertoire that spans the globe including classical masterworks, operatic arias, the sizzling energy of tangos, gypsy and folk songs, the group's theatrical stage presence and relaxed humor establishes an intimate rapport with audiences worldwide.

We had the pleasure of working together on numerous occasions and the audiences loved them!

Their numerous albums have played a huge role in the group's astonishing popularity, now having sales in the hundreds of thousands.

www.quartettogelato.ca

Picadinho à la Thiago

*My traditional Amazonian dish with ground beef, raisins and
capers — the idea is to have a nice balance
between sweet and sour.*

— Guadencio Thiago de Mello

SERVES 4 -6

INGREDIENTS

2 pounds / 900g choice ground beef

4 tablespoons raisins

6 teaspoons capers

A generous handful of fresh cilantro

2 medium onions, chopped

3 or 4 cloves fresh garlic

2-10 ounce / 250g cans Rotel diced tomatoes with green chillies

METHOD

Crush the cloves of garlic and sauté in olive oil. Once the garlic is brownish add the chopped onions and stir well. When the onions are translucent, add the ground beef gradually.

Brown the meat well, always stirring to break it up so that it is not lumpy as that affects the taste.

When the beef is nearly done, add the capers and raisins. Stir to make the raisins soft and allow the capers to add flavor to the beef.

Add cilantro and stir.

Once the beef is fully cooked add the tomatoes and turn off the heat. Make sure the tomatoes are soft but not crushed.

Serve with rice and black beans — Brazilian or Cuban style (very thick).

See also Thiago's Avocado shake, page 31 and Tapioca, page 240

JOURNEY TO THE AMAZON

THIAGO DE MELLO, SHARON ISBIN and I had a wonderfully adventurous journey to the Amazon in 2001 when they performed at the gorgeous Teatro Amazonas in Manaus, 800 miles up the river. We also spent some magical times further upriver at the world renowned tree top lodge, Ariau, in the heart of the Rain Forest.

Cheeky Monkey. One of the spider monkeys taking a nap in his hammock.

Thiago (left) with his nephew Rosario.

Encontro das Aquas — The Meeting of the Waters. Many locals in Manaus call this the 8th wonder of the world. This is where the two rivers — the Rio Negro, which is almost black, and the Amazon, which is almost yellow — meet. The confluence of the bodies of water is amazing as the colors don't mix.
All Photos: MPC

Ricky's Tender Back Ribs

— Rick Nelson

SERVES 4-6

INGREDIENTS

3 pounds / 1.3kg back ribs / baby back ribs

1 medium to large onion, sliced

Barbeque sauce (Sweet Baby James or your favorite)

½ cup / 125ml white vinegar

Salt and pepper to taste

METHOD

Preheat the oven to 325F / 160C

Place the ribs in the bottom of a roasting pan, add water
(not so much as to cover the ribs).

Add vinegar, onion, salt & pepper to taste.

Cover and bake for 1½ to 1¾ hours.

Carefully remove ribs and place on your grill (gas / charcoal).

Searing the bottom side first, depending on grill temperature,
cook 5-10 minutes each side.

Turn ribs over and baste the underside (now on top) with your favorite BBQ sauce
(Baby Jim's).

Again turn the ribs over and baste the top with sauce.

Continue cooking on the grill until done to perfection.

Carefully remove from the
grill (they'll be very tender
and may start to fall apart,
so be careful!)

Enjoy!

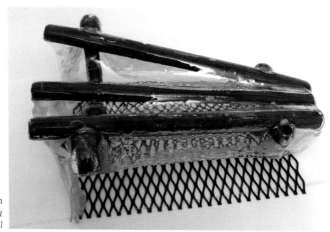

*See also Rick's Famous
Deviled Eggs, page 18*

Rick Nelson
Vitrident
Glass and Metal

Some photos by Rick Nelson from his
grand journey to Australia in 2001.

Trumpeter's Pork Tenderloin with Grilled Figs

My trips to Lafayette and to Virginia were some of my favorite musical and cultural experiences. Where else and with whom else could you share the best of classical, jazz, Cajun and Zydeco than in Michael's company. To play great chamber music and then eat Jambalaya and boogie down to the music of Zachary Richard is to live a richly rewarded life. Thank you Michael for your passion and dedication to life in the arts!

— Stephen Burns

SERVES 6

INGREDIENTS

2 Pork Tenderloins (1-3lbs / 1.3kg)

1 pound / 450g fresh figs (approximately 12)

Balsamic vinegar

1 whole lemon grated, zest included

¾ cup / 175ml fresh lemon juice

3 tablespoons extra virgin olive oil

2 tablespoons chopped garlic (4 cloves)

1½ tablespoons minced fresh rosemary

3 full rosemary sprigs

1 tablespoon chopped fresh thyme leaves

2 teaspoons Dijon mustard

Kosher salt

Freshly ground black pepper

Salt to taste

METHOD

Combine the lemon zest, lemon juice, ½ cup olive oil, garlic, rosemary, thyme, mustard, and 2 teaspoons salt in a sturdy 1-gallon resealable plastic bag. Add the pork tenderloins and turn to coat with the marinade. Squeeze out the air and seal the bag. Marinate the pork in the refrigerator for at least 3 hours but preferably overnight.

Preheat the oven to 400F / 200C

Remove the tenderloins from the marinade and discard the marinade but keep the herbs that cling to the meat. Sprinkle the tenderloins generously with salt and pepper. Heat the olive oil in a large oven-proof sauté pan over medium-high heat. Sear the pork tenderloins on all sides until golden brown. Place the sauté pan in the oven and roast the tenderloins for 10 to 15 minutes. Carve into ½-inch-thick diagonal slices. The thickest part of the tenderloin will be quite pink (it's just fine!) and the thinnest part will be well done. Season with salt and pepper and serve warm, or at room temperature with the juices that collect in the platter.

Slice the figs in half lengthwise, brush with olive oil and grill flesh side down on very hot iron grill until flesh is lightly charred. Turn to skin-side and grill until juices bubble. Reduce with balsamic vinegar until viscous.

Platter the loins flanked with figs, then drizzle with reduced balsamic vinegar and enjoy with an excellent Ribera del Duero.

Conductor, trumpet virtuoso, and composer STEPHEN BURNS is the Artistic Director of the Fulcrum Point New Music Project in Chicago. He has been acclaimed on four continents for his consistently and widely varied performances encompassing recitals, orchestral appearances, chamber ensemble engagements, and innovative multi-media presentations involving video, dance theatre, and sculpture. In 1988 he won First Prize at the Maurice André International Competition, which brought him numerous engagements, including a Paris recital, national television appearances and tours of Europe, Asia and the United States.

He has performed in the major concert halls of New York, Boston, Washington DC, Los Angeles, Houston, Vancouver, Hong Kong, Tokyo, Paris, and Venice and has performed at the White House and has appeared on NBC's *Today Show* and NPR's *All Things Considered*. In 1998 Stephen Burns was invited to create innovative new music programs as the Artist in Residence with Performing Arts Chicago. In the process he created the Fulcrum Point New Music Project and the American Concerto Orchestra whose mission it is to champion New Art Music influenced and inspired by Pop culture, World Music, literature, film, art, theatre, dance, nature, politics, and social dynamics.

A conducting student of Jorma Panula, Gerard Schwarz and Pinchas Zukerman, Mr. Burns often appears as both soloist and conductor performing in repertoire ranging from Bach and Haydn to works by Copland, Shostakovitch and André Jolivet. He has given numerous premières by American composers Rorem, David Stock, Gunther Schuller, Robert Rodriguez, and Philip Glass, as well as composers of international renown Stockhausen, Franck Amsellem, Somei Satoh, Aulis Sallinen. Stephen Burns is a frequent guest artist at many prestigious summer festivals including Santa Fe, Kuhmo, Tanglewood, Mostly Mozart, Spoleto, Caramoor, Lieksa, Ravinia, Grand Canyon, Moab, Estate Musicale St. Cecilia, and Divonne les Bains.

www.fulcrumpoint.org

Elisa's Ricotta Ravioli

This is a simple and almost foolproof recipe. It's great if you need an elegant dinner pulled together when you have no time, which is usually the case for me. My grandmother, who gave me this recipe, used to make her own fresh ravioli. I unfortunately did not inherit that particular talent!

— **Elisa Monte**

SERVES 4

INGREDIENTS

9 ounces / 225g spinach/ricotta ravioli

5 ounces / 140g baby spinach or arugula

5 or 6 fresh sage leaves, crushed

3 ounces / 75g butter

3 ounces / 100ml vegetable stock (can be divided half white wine and half stock)

7 ounces / 200g Parmigiana Reggiano, grated

Salt and black pepper to taste

METHOD

Boil salted water and cook the ravioli. Time will vary depending on if they are fresh — in which case 2 minutes — or dried, then read the directions on the box.

In a large saucepan bring the butter and stock to a high simmer. Add the sage leaves to infuse the sauce. Add the pasta, spinach and parmigiana. Mix together gently.

Be careful not to overcook the ravioli, you don't want the filling spilling out. Since there are so few ingredients, try to get the best quality of each. Good imported butter (I like French or Danish) and Reggiano parmigiana really are the best.

ELISA MONTE made her professional debut dancing with Agnes de Mille. She then became a Principal Dancer with such esteemed companies as the Martha Graham Dance Company, Lar Lubovitch and Pilobolus. Her first choreographic creation, *Treading* (1979) defined her as a leader in contemporary dance. Rooted in sensuality and controlled sustained energy, her unique choreographic style is daring, intense and passionate.

She cofounded and launched her own company in 1981 and still serves as Artistic Director. She has created more than 50 works which are now in the repertoire not only of her own company, Elisa Monte Dance, but also staged by the Boston Ballet, Alvin Ailey American Dance Theatre, San Francisco Ballet, Les Grands Ballets Canadiens, Philadanco, Contemporary Dance Company of South Africa and many other world class companies.

www.elisamontedance.org

RONN GUIDI established the Oakland Ballet in 1965 basing the company on the same principles that created the legendary Ballet Russes formed by Sergei Diaghilev in the early 20th century. Guidi inherited, as it were, the Ballets Russes traditions having studied under Raoul Pause and Adolf Bolm.

Under Ronn's leadership the Oakland Ballet staged highly acclaimed revivals of works by Michel Fokine, Anthony Tudor, Kurt Jooss and a host of other luminaries. His company also championed works of great American choreographers such as Agnes de Mille, Eugene Loring and Ruthanna Boris.

Ronn's Risotto à la Parmigiano

*This is an old family recipe from my Aunt Liavina
in Bergamo and it has been handed down
for generations. Always good for the soul.*

— Ronn Guidi

SERVES 4

INGREDIENTS

Olive Oil

1 medium onion, chopped

7 handfuls Arborio rice

1 glass white wine

2 cubes beef bouillon

1 cup / 100g parmesan cheese

METHOD

In a large black skillet warm the olive oil.

Add the chopped onion and cook for
2 minutes…be careful not to burn it.

Add the rice and mix well.

Then add the white wine.

When the wine has evaporated add boiling water.

Stir continuously and add the cubes of bouillon.

Add more water as needed to achieve a creamy consistency.

Finally add the cheese to the risotto and EAT.

Ahn's No Frills Saffron Risotto

My recipe is for a person like me who cannot cook complicated dishes. But I always get big compliments when I make this so you should try it. I have come a long way since I used to only know how to make drinks or coffee.

Once you have made this dish, keep in mind, you have made enough for 4 people. If your guests are Korean, however, you may well need to have more and more dishes coming. Koreans are like the Italians of Asia, eating and drinking are the single most important activities. Just ask our Mother who is an amazing chef who overfed my sisters and I our whole lives.

— **Maria Ahn & Ahn Trio**

SERVES 4

I AM NOT CALLING THIS RISOTTO MILANESE SINCE I DON'T USE BONE MARROW
(THAT'S TOO MUCH TO HANDLE FOR ME).

INGREDIENTS

2 cups / 250g Arborio or Carnaroli rice

1 medium onion, chopped. (I do this wearing a ski mask — very helpful. Swim goggles work well too)

5-6 cups / 1.25 organic low sodium chicken (or beef) stock

¾ teaspoon saffron threads

½ cup / 125ml good dry wine. Have more standing by. You might need to add some

4 tablespoons freshly grated Parmigiano-Reggiano – and more for serving later

¼ cup extra virgin olive oil

4 tablespoons panna (Italian cream) or 3 tablespoons crème fraiche. Alternatively you can use 2 tablespoons mascarpone — not totally authentic but it makes the texture creamier and sweeter which I love).

3 tablespoons unsalted butter

METHOD

In a large pot heat the stock. Set a timer for 25 minutes once it gets hot. (I like to set a timer, you don't have to). Turn the heat to low. Once it is boiled, set aside ½ cup / 125ml of the hot broth and add the saffron. You will use this later.

In a deep skillet cook the onion in 1 Tablespoon butter. After the butter is fully absorbed add 3 Tablespoons olive oil. Let the onions brown lightly over medium to high heat.

Add the rice, more olive oil as needed, letting the rice become coated — you are slightly toasting the rice so be careful not to let it burn. Now add the wine and cook until fully absorbed, adding another ¼ cup if needed.

Sisters Angella Ahn (violin), Maria (cello) and Lucia (piano) continue to redefine the art and architecture of chamber music, constantly drawing new audiences and commissioning new works. They thrive on breaking down barriers between different art forms and they frequently collaborate with dancers (including Nai-Ni Chen and the David Parsons Dance Company), electronic music artists, painters, photographers and even kite makers. Some of the visionary composers who have written for the Trio include Mark O'Connor, Kenji Bunch, Maurice Jarre and Michael Nyman. Born in Seoul, South Korea, the three sisters graduated from the Juilliard School of Music and have long been natural subjects for the international press. They have been featured in *TIME Magazine*, *People Magazine* among many others. Their enviable combination of talent and style keeps the Trio in high demand, performing and leading master classes throughout the world.

www.ahntrio.com

Have your favorite music like AHN TRIO'S *Lullaby for My Favorite Insomniac* playing; open a nice bottle of wine or your beverage of choice — you will want a sip or two while stirring and adding.

Add the stock one ladle at a time. Keep stirring, keep adding. You don't want the rice to stick to the bottom of the pan. After all the liquid is absorbed, add another ladle of stock and repeat.

Add the saffron-infused broth that you had previously set aside. By now you have been cooking for about 12 or 13 minutes. Keep stirring, keep adding one ladle at a time.

Add the panna or crème fraiche and keep stirring.

Add parmigiana and keep stirring.

Now you are ready to taste. You may like to add a little salt, but be conservative with salt.

Did the timer go off?

Taste again. It should be *al dente* but not hard. Once you are satisfied, fold the remaining butter into the rice and add salt if needed.

Cover and let sit for a minute or two. Serve warm with a side dish of more parmigiana.

Crabmeat Quiche &
Dijon Quiche Lorraine

— *Yolande deLadurantaye Snead*

CRAB MEAT QUICHE
SERVES 4-6

INGREDIENTS

3 large brown eggs

1 cups / 250ml heavy cream

¾ teaspoon coarse salt

1¼ cups / 150g grated Gruyère (or Swiss) cheese

½ pound / 225g crabmeat

1-8" pie shell

METHOD

Preheat the oven to 375F / 190C

Beat the eggs, cream and salt together. Combine the grated cheese and the crabmeat and spread evenly over the pie crust. Pour the eggs and cream mixture over the cheese and crabmeat and bake for 35-40 minutes until puffy and brown.

YOLANDE and her mother, Dee deLadurantaye at Maria's wedding at The American Theatre.

Dee served as the Executive Assistant to the Director of the Hampton Public Library for years and years. She was one of the staunchest supporters of the arts in Hampton. Yolande, born in New Orleans, enjoyed a lifelong career as a surgical technologist. And, as Maria so aptly states, "she is an awesome cook"!

DIJON QUICHE LORRAINE
SERVES 4-6

INGREDIENTS

1 ½ cups / 150g grated Swiss cheese

5 slices/rashers bacon, cooked, drained and crumbled

2 tablespoons green onions, chopped

3 large brown eggs, slightly beaten

1 cup / 250ml heavy cream

¼ cup / 60ml Dijon mustard

1-8" deep dish pie shell

METHOD

Preheat the oven to 375F / 190C

Layer the cheese, bacon and onions in the pie crust. In a small bowl, combine the eggs, cream and mustard. Pour evenly over the layers. Bake for 35-40 minutes until a knife inserted in the center of the pie comes out clean.

Ginger's Salmon Loaf with Pecan

Very easy to make and very delicious!
— Ginger Grace

SERVES 4

INGREDIENTS

1-1 pound / 450g can pink salmon, drained and flaked

2 cups / 250g bread crumbs, moistened

1 tablespoon onion chopped

1 tablespoon butter, melted

½ teaspoon salt

½ cup / 125ml milk

1 large brown egg, slightly beaten

METHOD

Preheat the oven to 350F / 180C

In a bowl, combine salmon, crumbs, onion, butter and salt. In a separate bowl, combine egg and milk. Add to salmon mixture and mix thoroughly. Shape into a loaf on a greased shallow baking pan or a 2½" deep long pan. Bake for 35 to 40 minutes.

TOPPING

½ cup / 64g Pecans, (finely chopped)

A generous handful dill weed

1 Lemon

Heat up the pecans with olive oil in frying pan, until crispy. Sprinkle on top of the salmon along with Dill weed. Squeeze lemon juice on top to flavor. Makes for a crispy topping!

Photo: Gerry Goodstein

See also Ginger's recipe for Sweet & Sour Cabbage Soup, page 51

In a role that she has definitely made her own, GINGER GRACE continues to star and tour coast to coast in the wonderful production of *The Belle of Amherst*. In this engaging, absorbing and highly entertaining portrait of the legendary Emily Dickinson, Ginger brings to life American's most beloved and most eccentric poet. Encapsulating what theatre is all about, the production transports audiences into Dickinson's home where life and poetry are interwoven.

www.thebelleofamherst.com

Alessio's Sea Urchin Spaghetti

*Spaghetti ai ricci, sea urchin spaghetti, uni pasta,
call it as you wish, but this dish has been a long time favorite
of mine and of my guests whether they were obsessively in
love with sea urchin or whether they previously despised
it — this very simple dish seems to always do the trick.*

— *Alessio Bax*

SERVES 4

INGREDIENTS

1 large box of Santa Barbara sea urchin (I recommend the Lobster Place, if in New York, at Chelsea Market. A bit pricey, but consistently good quality. You can look elsewhere for better deals, but be careful!)

½ bunch of chives

½ bunch of Italian flat parsley

1 clove garlic

250 grams of De Cecco spaghetti (my favorite, as they hold "al dente" perfectly well. I wouldn't waste time or money in fancier brands for this dish)

4-5 tablespoons of extra virgin olive oil

METHOD

Boil a large pot of salted water and cook the pasta. It should be firm to the bite, but not crunchy. Salt to taste. It needs to taste good enough to be eaten on its own. Also you won't be cooking this in any sauce, so it needs to be boiled to the final firmness. Save same pasta water for the sauce.

While boiling the pasta, heat the oil with the peeled, but not crushed (!), garlic clove. As soon as it starts to sizzle, turn it off and toss away the garlic, or it will overpower the sauce.

In a large metal bowl, pour most of the sea urchin, saving four or more pieces for decoration. Add the oil, the super finely chopped chives and chopped parsley and start whipping it with a fork.

Add the cooked pasta as soon as it's ready. I like to use tongs to pull it out straight from the boiling pot, which will have the added benefit of including some pasta water.

Keep whipping the whole thing with a fork for a few seconds until it is amalgamated into a creamy texture. If it seems too dry, add a bit of the pasta water.

Serve the pasta in four bowls and decorate with the pieces of sea urchin, with a little fresh chives and parsley.

Alessio with his wife, pianist Lucille Chung.
Photo: Lisa-Marie Mazzucco

My sea urchin spaghetti was photographed by Bonjwing Lee of *The Ulterior Epicure*, and mentioned in *The New York Times' Diner's Journal* by Jeff Gordiner. I have made it at home for lots and lots of musicians, friends and food lovers.

No big secret in this recipe, except for cooking perfectly the pasta, and getting the freshest Santa Barbara sea urchin. I love the rich creaminess of the Santa Barbara sea urchin, which somehow magically creates a creamy sauce, very much like a carbonara (don't ever think about adding cream to either dishes!!)

It is a very rich dish, so small portions are recommended.

See also Alessio's recipes for Bucatini, page 98, and Tiramisu, page 241

www.alessiobax.com

Captain Les' Toad in the Hole

This dish, a centuries old tradition in the U.K. is best served with a meaty gravy and steamed potatoes and vegetables of your choice.

— Les J. Mumford

INGREDIENTS

8 thin pork sausages (chipolatas)

1 tablespoon vegetable oil

2 cups plain flour

4 large brown eggs

1 cup of milk

Salt & pepper to taste

METHOD

Preheat oven to 400F / 200C

Pour oil into a metal baking dish and arrange sausages on top in a single layer.

Bake for 10 minutes in preheated oven.

Meanwhile, in a medium bowl, add flour, make a well in the center of the flour and add eggs and half the milk. Whisk together until smooth and then gradually add the remaining milk until the batter is smooth. Season with salt and pepper.

Remove sausages from the oven and ladle the batter over them until the sausages are almost covered.

Return to oven and bake for 35 minutes or until the batter has risen and is a nice golden brown.

CAPTAIN L. J. MUMFORD served as an Officer in the Royal Regiment of Artillery in Europe, Scandinavia and South East Asia before retiring in the rank of Captain when he moved to Australia. In Sydney, his civilian career encompassed several appointments as CEO of large companies before he established his own consulting firm.

Our paths first crossed in 1967 when Les was the Duty Officer of his regiment in Germany. He recalls: "I received a message that 6 British schoolboys were stranded nearby because arrangements for their care and accommodations had fallen through. I picked the boys up and made the arrangements for them to stay the night at the barracks. The following day I was instructed by my Commanding Officer to take the hapless boys under my wing and keep them amused and occupied for the remainder of their two week stay. One of the schoolboys was Michael Curry and over that 2 week period we forged a friendship that lasts to this day."

Julie's Zucchini Bake

*This delicious recipe was passed down to me from my
Aunt and as she always liked to say it is luscious!*

— Julie Calzone

SERVES 4-6

INGREDIENTS

2 pounds / 900g sliced zucchini

4 tablespoons onions, chopped

1-10 ounce / 290g can cream of mushroom or cream of chicken soup

1 cup / 250ml sour cream

1 cup / 130g shredded raw carrots

8 ounces / 200g Pepperidge Farm stuffing mix

½ cup / 100g butter, melted

METHOD

Preheat oven to 350F / 180C

Boil the zucchini and onions in 1 cup water for about 5 minutes. Drain.

Combine the undiluted soup, sour cream and carrots. Add the zucchini and onions.

In a separate bowl, toss the stuffing mix with the butter. Spread half of this mixture in a 13" x 9" dish.

Spoon the vegetable mixture over the stuffing and sprinkle the remaining stuffing on top.

Jackson Square, New Orleans. *Photo: MPC*

See also Honey Drop Cookies, page 219 and Pfeffernusse, page 229

JULIE CALZONE has been running a highly successful advertising agency (Calzone and Associates) in Lafayette, Louisiana for more than 30 years. Her list of clients includes some of the leading businesses and industries in the region. Julie is also an accomplished horsewoman, and we spent many a day together doing dressage and taking riding lessons.

Justin's Tonkatsu

This was one of Justin's favorite meals as he was growing up. But he ALWAYS puts Shoyu (soy sauce) on his rice; that is a classic "no-no" in Japan. His other favorite was Hamburger Stroganoff with ground beef (we were always on a budget with 5 kids). He prefers real sour cream as opposed to the plain yogurt I always used.

— Phyllis (For Justin) Kauflin

SERVES 8-10

TONKATSU = JAPANESE FOR PORK (TON) CUTLET (KATSU)

INGREDIENTS

3-4 pounds / 1.8kg boneless pork loin

3 large brown eggs

2 tablespoons cold water

½-¾ cup / 100g unbleached flour

2-3 cups / 380g panko bread crumbs

METHOD

Slice the pork loin into desired thickness — thinner if you have a lot of guests!

Lightly whisk the eggs in the water — add more water if needed to "stretch".

Season the flour with salt and ground pepper.

Lightly dredge the pork slices in the flour; dip into the egg mixture and then dredge in the breadcrumbs.

Deep fry for about 2 minutes per slice or pan fry in about 1 inch peanut oil, turning when golden. Lately I have been using the wok.

Once golden, set aside the pork on a cookie sheet and keep warm by covering with foil. When cooking large batches, after all the slices are done, pop into the oven for about 10 minutes to reheat.

Serve over rice with fresh spinach and garlic stir fry, fresh applesauce, sliced cabbage with soy and lemon.

Photo: Rory Anderson

Photo: Tony Cenicola, The New York Times

A rising superstar on the international jazz scene, pianist and composer JUSTIN KAUFLIN began performing at the age of 6, on the violin. After losing his sight, he learned 5 grades of Braille and switched to jazz piano studied at the Governors School for the Arts and began performing professionally, notably with the Jae Sinnett Trio, at the age of 16.

He graduated at the top of his class from Salem High School and received a Presidential Scholarship to attend William Patterson University in New Jersey. There he was taken under the wings of legendary trumpeter Clark Terry and performed in the Clark Terry Ensemble. In 2008 he graduated summa cum laude and moved to New York City and, at the age of 23, produced, led, composed and performed his first CD, *Introducing Justin Kauflin*. At the same time, his relationship with Clark Terry was documented by Absolute Clay Productions. Five years in the making, *Keep on Keepin' On* won both the Heineken Audience and Best New Director at the Tribeca Film Festival. The documentary was also shortlisted for an Oscar for best documentary film in 2015.

He subsequently signed with renowned producer and music icon Quincy Jones and in 2013 Justin joined Quincy on tours to Switzerland, Austria, France, South Korea and Japan. In 2014 he released his second CD, *Dedication* which consists of 12 original compositions, 9 of which Justin dedicated to his mentors, family and friends. The album debuted at #10 on Billboard's Traditional Jazz Chart and remained in the top 10 for 9 straight weeks.

In addition to touring the world, Justin is always working on new compositions and ideas.
www.justinkauflin.com

Larry Vanover
The American Theatre
Oil on Board
Collection of the Author

Act III

Desserts

Anya's ALMOND COOKIES

Kevin & Cindy's FRIED APPLES

Vadim's RUM APPLE PUFF TART

Caroline & Stephen's APPLE ALMOND CAKE

Gil's Aunt Jean's APPLE PECAN CAKE

Miles & Susan's APPLE WALNUT CAKE

Sally's SPIRIT FREE BANANAS FOSTER

Stephen's BANOFFEE PIE

Mick's BLANCMANGE

Deborah's CRANBERRY PEACH COBBLER

Susan's CAPUCCINO CRÈME BRULEE

Rob's FANTASTY FUDGE

JoAnn Falletta's FAMILY CHEESECAKE

Felicity's BAKED LEMON CHEESECAKE

Felicity's SOUR CREAM CHOCOLATE CAKE

Nicki's CHOCOLATE CAKE

Grandma McCutcheon's COCONUT CRÈME PIE

Maria Paranova's COFFEE FLAN

Betty Buckley's STUFFED DATE DROP COOKIES

Malcolm's FIFTEENS

Jude's "FRIED EGG PIE"

Letia's GINGER SNAPS

Kacey's HARLEQUIN PINWHEELS

Beth's HAZLENUT TRIANGLES

Mommie's MILE HIGH ICE CREAM PIE

Julie's HONEY DROPS

Gloria's Aunt Betty's KOLACHES

Leisa's JELLY SLICE

Sharon's MANGO BLUEBERRY PIE

Thea & Peter's NORTH COUNTRY PARKIN (Gingerbread)

Chef Bobby's KAHLUA PECAN PIE

Julie's PFEFFERNISSE

Sherri's PINEAPPLE BREAD CASSEROLE

Eric's PISTACCHIO PANNA COTTO

Bonnie's ROLY-POLY & WHISKY CREAM

Linda's Rosemary SHORTBREAD

Grandma Eddy's SHOO FLY PIE

Wadsworth Family's SWEET POTATO PIE

Thiago's MINGAU de TAPIOCA

Alessio's TIRAMISU

Anya's Almond Cookies

Anya, my daughter, makes these cookies often for the family and they are absolutely fabulous. No butter or dairy of any kind but simply delicious. Great for vegans/vegetarians like me who want a treat every now and then. Enjoy!

— Colin Carr

INGREDIENTS

1 cup / 128g toasted ground almonds

1 cup / 128g ground oats

1 cup / 128g all purpose flour

½ teaspoon baking powder

½ teaspoon cinnamon

¼ teaspoon salt

½ cup / 125ml vegetable oil

½ cup / 125ml rice syrup or honey

1 teaspoon of grated lemon zest

½ teaspoon vanilla

¼ cup of jam — your choice of apricot, strawberry or raspberry or even blackberry.

METHOD

Preheat oven to 350F / 180C

Combine with a wooden spoon almonds, oats, flour, baking powder, cinnamon and salt in medium sized bowl, set aside.

Mix oil, rice syrup, lemon zest and vanilla in large bowl with a wooden spoon.

Combine dry and wet ingredients.

Spoon balls of dough onto greased baking trays and flatten.

With your thumb, imprint each cookie, making a small well in each one.

Place a tablespoon jam into the wells.

Bake for 15-20 minutes.

A Fellow of The Royal Academy of Music, COLIN CARR is in great demand internationally as a recitalist, chamber musician, soloist with major orchestras and recording artist. The list of conductors with whom he has worked is astonishing: Sir Simon Rattle, Charles Dutoit, Sir Neville Marriner and many others. He has been a regular guest at the BBC Proms Concerts in the Royal Albert Hall. With his duo partner, Thomas Sauer, he has toured the U.S. and Europe, recently being featured at the Royal Concertgebouw, Philadelphia's Chamber Music Society and at Wigmore Hall in London. His recordings of the Bach Suites and the unaccompanied works of Kodaly, Britten, Crumb and Schuller are highly acclaimed. As a member of the Golub Kaplan Carr Trio, Colin recorded and toured the world for more than twenty years.

He is a frequent guest at the world's leading festivals and a regular guest with the Emerson and Guarneri Quartets as well as with the Chamber Music Society of Lincoln Center.

The winner of many prestigious competitions and awards, Colin has been a Professor at the Royal Academy since 1998 and has also served on the faculty at the New England Conservatory.

We have had the pleasure of working together on many occasions — first when he won the Young Concert Artists International Auditions and then with the Golub Kaplan Carr Trio and then again as a soloist in a stunning performance of the Bach Cello Suites.

www.colincarr.net

Cindy & Kevin's Fried Apples

Every time I make these, sweet memories of apple picking trips with my aunt come flooding back. This is a true Southern dish. When I was a little girl, my Aunt Agnes would take me apple picking. I loved it! There was an older lady who had several apple trees and she was so sweet to allow us to pick them. Of course we would pick a bunch for her too. We would load up baskets of apples and off we would go. We eat them with whipped cream or ice cream. I will always cherish the amazing aromas from the kitchen when Aunt Agnes was cooking these.

— *Cindy Spencer*

SERVES 4

INGREDIENTS

3 or 4 apples cored and sliced (skin on or off ... Your choice) I leave it on! I've tried many kinds of Apples ... Choose your favorite!

1-2 tablespoons butter

⅓ cup / 50g brown sugar

1 teaspoon cinnamon

METHOD

Melt the butter in a medium sized skillet. Add sliced apples, sugar, and cinnamon.

Simmer over medium heat until bubbly. Continue cooking for about 10-20 minutes, depending on how thick you cut your Apples.

Cook until tender.

Enjoy!!

KEVIN AND CINDY SPENCER, creators of The Theatre of Illusion, have dedicated their lives to making a difference in communities around the world — both on and off the stage.

Winners of multiple honors and awards, they were named Performing Arts Entertainers of the Year no fewer than six times and won the coveted Merlin Award for International Magicians of the Year. Kevin is an innovator, educator, researcher, consultant, speaker and curriculum designer as well as an acclaimed film producer.

We all became fast friends, along with McIver the dog, when they first packed the house. Their show became a regular favorite on the schedule and Kevin has led several week-long magic camps there in the past few years.

HocusFocusEducation.com

Vadim's Rum Apple Puff Tart

*Warning…this tart is gone before you can
even manage to say: Bon Appétit!!!*

— Vadim Gluzman

INGREDIENTS

1 package puff pastry dough

5 big apples

2-3 tablespoons apricot jam

½ lemon

2 tablespoons butter

1 tablespoon brown sugar

Rum

METHOD

Preheat oven to 400 F / 220C

Sprinkle baking sheet with cooking spray. Place puff pastry dough on the sheet.

Peel your apples, remove the cores and slice them into thin equal slices. Squeeze half of lemon on the apples.

Place your apple slices diagonally on the baking sheet, starting with the largest diagonal in the center of the rectangle and working your way out.

Sprinkle the sugar and add the bits of butter over the top of your apples.

Bake for 35-40 min, rotating the pan once half way through until pastry is puffed and apples are golden.

After the tart has finished baking, mix apricot jam and rum together. Brush this on top of the tart (while hot) for a nice shiny finish.

Serve warm.

Photo: Marco Borggreve

VADIM'S extraordinary artistry on the violin brings to life the gloriously virtuostic traditions of the 19th and 20th centuries. A native of the former Soviet Union, he regularly appears as guest soloist with The Chicago, London, San Francisco Symphonies as well as the London, Israel, Munich Philaharmonic Orchestrsas, among many others. He has collaborated with such maestros as Neeme Jarvi, Michael Tilson Thomas, Andrew Litton, Semyon Bychkov, Itzhak Perlman and Rafael Fruhbeck de Burgos. In the past season, he made guest appearances with Chirstoph von Dohnanyi and Ricardo Chailly. He also appeared in solo recital in major capitals including London and Jerusalem and led performances with the Moscow Virutosi, Sinfonietta Cracovia and the Vancouver Symphony. He and his wife, acclaimed pianist Angela Yoffe founded and direct the widely acclaimed North Shore Chamber Music Festival in Northbrook, Illnois.

www.vadimgluzman.com

Caroline & Stephen's Apple Almond Cake

*This is a lovely dessert that we have
enjoyed for years…hope you do, too.*

— Caroline Brown

SERVES 6-8

INGREDIENTS

5 ounces / 125g melted butter or margarine

2 large brown eggs

8 ounces / 225g sugar

1 teaspoon almond essence

1 teaspoon baking powder

8 ounces / 225g self-rising flour

10 ounces / 250g cooking apples (peeled and sliced)

1 ounce / 25g flaked almonds

METHOD

Preheat oven to 325F / 160C

Mix all of the ingredients (except the apples and flaked almonds)
together until it is smooth and resembles a thick paste.

Place half the mixture (It rises so it won't be a very thick layer)
on the bottom of an 8" or 9" square tin lined with greaseproof / wax paper.

Layer the apples on top.

Spoon the remaining cake mix in dollops over the cake mix.

Sprinkle the almonds over the top.

Bake in the middle of the oven for 1-1¼ hours until golden brown.

Cellist Caroline Brown founded the Hanover Band, one of the world's pre-eminent period instrument orchestras in 1980. Known especially for the excellence of performance and recordings of 18th and 19th century music, the players in the Band are amongst the best in their field.

The orchestra's impressive catalogue of more than 175 CD's includes the award winning Beethoven cycle, *Donizetti's Lucia di Lammermoor*, the Bach *Brandenburg Concertos* and many more.

The Hanover Band's list of directors/conductors over the years includes such legends as Sir Charles Mackerras, Monica Huggett, Roy Goodman, Anthony Halstead, Nicholas McGegan and a host of others.

Caroline and her husband and manager of the Band, Stephen, and I first met in 1990 we subsequently worked together on many glorious concerts for several years.

Aunt Jean's Apple Pecan Cake

My Aunt Jean was a great Southern cook. Her food was always hearty and soulful. On Saturdays, she would cook lots of food, usually straight out of her garden. Folks would come around, visit and eat. It was all about family, community, spending time with one another and, of course, great food. This has always been one of my favorites.

— Gil Hunter

SERVES 8-10

INGREDIENTS

2 cups / 250g sugar

3 large brown eggs

1½ cups / 375ml vegetable oil

¼ cup / 175ml orange juice

3 cups / 475g all-purpose flour

1 teaspoon baking soda

¼ teaspoon salt

1 tablespoon ground cinnamon

1 tablespoon vanilla extract

3 cups / 475g peeled and finely chopped green apples

1 cup / 130g chopped pecans

SAUCE

½ cup / 115g butter

1 cup / 130g brown sugar

½ cup / 125ml milk

½ teaspoon baking soda

METHOD

Preheat the oven to 325F / 160C Generously grease a bundt pan.

In a large bowl, combine the sugar, eggs, oil, orange juice, flour, baking soda, salt, cinnamon and vanilla extract; mix well. Fold apples and pecans into batter. Pour the batter into the bundt pan and bake approximately 1½ hours (Check by sticking a fork in the cake. The cake is done when the fork comes out clean).

For the sauce, melt the butter in a large saucepan. Stir in the brown sugar, milk, and baking soda. Bring to a boil, stirring constantly. Boil for 1 minute. Pour the sauce over the hot cake in the pan as soon as you remove it from the oven. Let stand 1 hour, then turn out onto a large plate. Aunt Jean's Apple Cake was very rich!

At the age of seven, GIL travelled with his family singing gospel music at churches, schools and community events. He has toured nationwide in productions such as *A Closer Walk with Patsy Cline, Big River, Cabaret* and *House at Pooh Corner*. He is now working on record production in New York with producer Tony Mack.

Gil came to the American Theatre on several occasions with the ever popular productions of Springer Theatre which is based in Columbus, Georgia.

Gil Hunter on ReverbNation.com

Miles & Susan's Apple Walnut Cake

Susan knows how much I love her apple walnut cake and she often has one waiting for me when I return from out of town. It makes coming home even more delicious! This cake is fabulous for breakfast, tea, dessert or topped with ice cream, etc.

— Miles Hoffman

SERVES 6

INGREDIENTS

2 large peeled and diced Granny Smith apples

¾ cup / 96g sugar

¼ cup / 60ml oil

1 large brown egg, beaten

1 cup / 130g all-purpose flour

1 teaspoon cinnamon

1 teaspoon baking soda

¼ teaspoon salt

1 teaspoon vanilla

½-1 cup / 125g chopped walnuts (nuts are essential in this recipe)

METHOD

Preheat the oven to 350F / 180C

Combine the peeled apples and sugar and let stand for at least 30 minutes.

Add remaining ingredients. (There will appear to be very little batter for the amount of apples — no worries!).

Put into a well-greased 8-inch square baking pan (or line the pan with parchment paper or nonstick foil). Bake for about 36 minutes.

FOR A LARGER CAKE

Use a lined or well-greased 9" x 13" pan. Double all of the ingredients except the baking soda. Leave baking soda at 1 teaspoon Bake 41 minutes.

Known to millions as the NPR *Morning Edition* music commentator, MILES HOFFMAN is the author of *The NPR Classical Music Companion*, which is now in its 10th printing!

He established The American Chamber Players in 1985 from a core group of artists of The Library of Congress Summer Chamber Festival. The American Chamber Players are the resident ensemble at the Kreeger Museum in Washington, DC. Hailed throughout the world, the ensemble performs repertoire ranging from familiar masterpieces to neglected gems to newly commissioned American works.

They have toured throughout North America, engaged and re-engaged by prestigious concert series from Florida to British Columbia, and they have traveled to Paris for a series of special gala concerts at the Paris Opéra and the Bibliothèque Nationale.

The American Chamber Players have recorded music of Mozart, Bruch, Bloch, Stravinsky, Harbison, and Rochberg for a series of compact discs and cassettes distributed internationally on the Koch International Classics label.

www.ACPlayers.com

Sally's Spirit Free Bananas Foster

Bananas Foster has always been my favorite dessert.
Be sure that the bananas are not too ripe or too green.
I love making this recipe.. When I stopped consuming
alcohol years ago I knew I could make a dessert
with the same taste and WOW... It is always a hit.

— *Sally Brown Perry*

SERVES 4

INGREDIENTS

4 medium ripe bananas

1 tablespoon butter

1 tablespoon raw turbinado sugar

Half of one fresh lemon

METHOD

Heat the butter on medium in a black skillet.

Slice the bananas into quarters and fry until golden brown.

Quickly add the sugar and as it melts, add the lemon.

Serve over a pound cake or with vanilla ice cream.

Photo: Jim Turner

SALLY BROWN PERRY, second from right, also known as Swami-Ma or Spirit Medicine is a Native American visionary and healer of Cherokee lineage. She leads sweat lodges, spirit medicine wheels, vision quests and world peace dances worldwide. From her retreat, the East West Bridge in Virgina she works with the revered Hindu teacher Swami Pamananad in aiding children, the homeless and those in need of medical attention. She has written two highly acclaimed books and is in constant demand as a lecturer and teacher.

www.sallyperry.net

Stephen's Banoffee Pie

This is one of my most favorite and delicious memory recipes.
My sister perfected this dish and passed it on to me.

— Stephen Beagley

SERVES 4-6

INGREDIENTS

4 ounces / 100g butter

25 / 250g digestive biscuits

4 ounces / 100g dark brown sugar

1-12 ounce can / 379g condensed milk

TOPPINGS

4 small bananas

1 cup / 284ml carton double cream

One or two Cadbury's Flake candy bars (if you can find them)

Cocoa powder

METHOD

To make the base crush the biscuits until they are like very fine crumbs then tip into a bowl. Stir in the melted butter,and then press the mixture into the base and one and a half inch up the sides of a baking pan. Chill the base while making the filling.

Place the butter and sugar into a non stick saucepan over a low heat stirring until the butter melts and the sugar dissolves; add the milk and slowly bring to the boil. Keep stirring to make the caramel and as soon as it thickens remove from the heat. Spread the filling over your chilled base and leave till cool and then chill in the fridge for about an hour or when firm to the touch.

TOPPINGS: Slice the bananas and fold half of them into the cream and spoon the mixture over the toffee base; decorate with the rest of the bananas, chocolate flakes and dust with cocoa powder.

STEPHEN BEAGLEY started his ballet training at the age of 8 and a year later joined the Royal Ballet School. He graduated into the company at 17 and served as Principal Dancer for many years. He had the honor of having ballets created on him by such legends as Fredrick Ashton, Kenneth Macmillan, David Bintley, John Neumeir, Glen Tetley and Ashley Page. As Principal he dances of all of the major roles in the Company.

In 1984 he played the lead in *Cats* and then toured Italy as Rocky in *The Rocky Horror Picture Show*. He then completed two seasons of *The Hot Shoe Show* for BBC Television. He also played the role of Tom Thumb in the musical *Barnum* and was a member of the Royal Shakespeare Company in their production of *A Clockwork Orange*.

Stephen is now Artistic Director of the Bangkok City Ballet and a guest teacher at the English National Ballet. He regularly teaches for such other companies as the Boston Ballet, Scottish Ballet, Hong Kong Ballet and many others.

Mick's Blancmange
That is Bluh-monge

Michael and I were at college together in the early 1970s and had a weekly evening of fun — laundering in the 'Washerama', and cooking in turns. There was a fish casserole which we counted as a favorite, and a blancmange would be produced from time to time. It was easy to do once you got used to it. We would drink cider or cheap wine and write poetry, forgetting about the mountain of course work we were meant to be doing.

— **Mick Escott**

SERVES 4

INGREDIENTS

1.5 ounces / 40g cornstarch or cornflour

2-3 tablespoons sugar

1 pint / 500ml milk

Flavoring (raspberry, vanilla, lemon, orange, chocolate, all good)

METHOD

Blend together the cornflour, sugar and 2 tablespoons cold milk taken from the pint.

Warm the rest of the milk and pour onto the mixed cornflour, stirring well.

Return to the heat and add the flavorings. Bring to the boil and simmer for one minute, stirring all the time.

Pour into a wetted mould and leave to set in a cool place.

To stop skin forming, sprinkle a little sugar on the blancmange while it is setting.

FLAVORS

Raspberry or soft fruits — add ½ teaspoon

Vanilla — add half a teaspoon vanilla essence to recipe;

Lemon — add grated rind of 1 lemon or lemon juice to recipe;

Orange — replace some of the milk with orange cordial or concentrated juice;

Chocolate — add cocoa powder to taste to recipe.

The author of 3 books and a fully qualified accountant, MICK ESCOTT served as Treasurer at the Bristol Old Vic Theatre and School and before that at the Victoria Theatre, Stoke on Trent. He is also a trustee of the Shakespeare at the Tobacco Factory and free lance consultant.

www.mickescott.co.uk

Deborah's Cranberry Peach Cobbler

*Here is one of my family's longtime favorites and
it is easy to make and very very tasty.*

— Deborah Thorpe

INGREDIENTS

½ cup / 64g fresh cranberries

1-16 ounce / 450g can of peaches or
2½ cups fresh peaches

½ cup / 64g sugar

1 tablespoon flour

Juice of one fresh lemon

TOPPING

½ cup / 64g quick oats

½ cup / 120g butter-melted

½ cup / 64g flour

⅓ cup / 30g brown sugar

METHOD

Preheat the oven to 350F / 180C

Toss peaches and cranberries with lemon and sugar and spread in pie dish.

Mix topping ingredients and spread on top of fruit mixture.

Bake for 30-40 minutes.

DEBORAH THORPE is Assistant Director/Foundation Director at the Governor's Magnet School of the Arts in Norfolk, VA. She earned her BA degree in Dance and Education from Goucher College and her M.Ed degree in Dance Education from Colorado State University. Her professional modern dance career ranged from regional dance companies in Colorado, Baltimore and New York City. In 1984 she assisted in forming GSA, and from 1985- 2011 she was Chair of the GSA Dance Department. She has been an integral part of the arts community in Hampton Roads and has served as a panel member for the Virginia Commission on the Arts, was President of the Board for Todd Rosenlieb Dance for 8 years, currently serves on the Board of Directors for the Downtown Norfolk Council, is a member of WHRO Community Advisory Board, and is a member of the Horizon Circle of CHKD. She is the Founding Director of the Regional High School Dance Festival and received the Outstanding Service Award from the National High School Dance Festival in 2002.

www.gsarts.net

Susan's Cappuccino Crème Brulée

*These can be made two days in advance of serving
as long as they are kept covered and chilled.*

— Susan Stapleton McLaurin

SERVES 4

INGREDIENTS

1 cup / 250ml heavy cream

1cup / 250ml milk

⅓ cup / 30g granulated sugar

1 tablespoon instant
expresso powder

Two 2-inch cinnamon sticks

4 large egg yolks

2 tablespoons firmly packed
dark brown sugar

METHOD

Susan Stapleton McLaurin, *Waiting for Coffee*, *Mixed media*

Preheat the oven to 325F / 160C

In a small saucepan combine the cream & milk with half the granulated sugar, the expresso powder, and the cinnamon sticks and heat over moderately low heat, stirring occasionally, until it is hot. In a smaller bowl whisk together the yolks and the remaining granulated sugar and add the milk mixture in a stream, whisking. Remove the cinnamon sticks and combine well.

Divide the custard among four ⅔ cup ramekins set in a baking pan, add enough hot water to the pan to reach halfway up the sides of the ramekins, and bake the custards in the middle of the oven for 40 minutes, or until they are just set. Remove from the pan, let the custards cool, and chill them, covered, for at least 4 hours. Blot dry the tops with paper towels and sprinkle them evenly with brown sugar. Put the custards under a preheated broiler about 1 inch from the heat, turning them to caramelize the sugar evenly and being careful not to let the sugar burn, for 2 minutes.

See also Susan's recipe for Lasagna, page 142

www.susanmclaurin.com

Rob's Fantasy Fudge

Here is my grandmother Delta Futral's (great southern name) fudge recipe. She made this every Christmas my entire childhood and when she passed away I had my sister continue the tradition. It's amazing.

— **Robert W. Cross**

SERVES 4-6

INGREDIENTS

3 cups / 375g sugar

¾ cup / 170g butter

⅔ cup / 6 ounce / 175ml can evaporated milk

12 ounces / 300g semisweet chocolate pieces

1-7 ounce / 175g jar marshmallow crème

1 cup / 128g chopped nuts (walnuts, pecans or mixed)

1 teaspoon vanilla

METHOD

Combine sugar, butter and milk in a saucepan. Bring to a rolling boil, stirring constantly. Boil 5 minutes over medium heat stirring constantly (be careful — the mixture scorches easily). Remove from heat. Stir in chocolate pieces until melted. Add marshmallow crème, nuts and vanilla and beat until well blended. Pour into a greased 13" x 9" pan. Cool and cut into squares.

Photo: David Polston

ROB and I collaborated on the first two Virginia International Arts Festivals and had a great time. A graduate of the New England Conservatory, Rob has been Principal Percussionist in the Virginia Symphony since 1987. He joined the orchestra in 1981 and has also served as Personnel Manager, Artistic Administrator, Orchestra Manager and Interim Executive Director. As Director of the Virginia Arts Festival he continues to bring the most revered artists in the world to the Southeastern Virginia region. www.vaartsfest

Joann Falletta's Family Cheesecake

Here is the Falletta family cheesecake recipe.
Not healthy but quite delicious!

The cheesecake generally tastes even better if it is not refrigerated so I typically make it the day before it is going to be served and let it cool naturally. Leftovers must be refrigerated for later use.

— Joann Falletta

SERVES 6

INGREDIENTS

2 pounds / 900g cream cheese

¼ pound / 113g sweet butter

1½ cups / 190g sugar

3 tablespoons flour

3 tablespoons cornstarch

1 tablespoon pure vanilla extract

4 large brown eggs

1 pint/500ml sour cream

METHOD

Preheat oven to 325F / 160C

Grease and flour cheesecake pan (springform pan: 9" inches).

Cream all ingredients (except sour cream) with a mixer until smooth.

Add sour cream and mix.

Bake for 1 hour in center of the oven.

Turn up the heat to low broil for just a minute or two at the end to add color to the top of the cake. Watch carefully so it doesn't burn!!

Remove cake from oven and let it cool. To prevent the top from cracking you might want to place the pan on trivets supporting the perimeter.

Acclaimed by *The New York Times* as "one of the finest conductors of her generation" JOANN FALLETTA is Music Director of the Buffalo Philharmonic and has just entered her 26th season as Conductor & Music Director of The Virginia Symphony. She also serves as Principal Guest Conductor of the Brevard Music Center and Music Advisor to the Hawaii Symphony.

She regularly appears with the world's finest orchestras and recently completed a 13 city tour with Sir James Galway and the Irish Chamber Orchestra. In North America, JoAnn has guest conducted well over 100 orchestras including those of Philadelphia, Los Angeles, San Francisco, Dallas, Montreal, Toronto and the National Symphony in Washington, D.C. In Europe she has appeared with the London Symphony, the Liverpool and Rotterdam Philharmonics, the BBC Scottish, Shanghai and China National Symphonies. Her summer festival appearances have included the Aspen, Wolf Trap, Tanglewood, Hollywood Bowl and OK Mozart Festivals, among others.

She has recorded dozens of albums and her discography currently included more than 90 titles. Her recording with the Buffalo Philharmonic and soprano Hila Plitmann of John Corigliano's *Mr. Tambourine Man* received 2 Grammy Awards. A longtime and dedicated champion of American orchestral music, Maestro Falletta will lead the Virginia Symphony in the world première of a Kenneth Fuchs' piece based on the works of poet Judith Wolf.

www.joannfalletta.com

Felicity's Baked Lemon Cheesecake

A delightful dessert.
— Felicity Ryan

SERVES 6-8

INGREDIENTS

1 pound / 490g prepared short crust pastry (or do your own)

¼ pint / 125ml mayonnaise

8 ounces / 200g cream cheese

3 ounces / 75g sugar

2 large brown eggs, separated

Grated rind of 2 lemons and a little juice

1 teaspoon vanilla essence

Confectioner's / Icing Sugar to sift over the cheesecake

METHOD

Pre heat oven to 350F / 180C

Roll out pastry, bake blind for 6-10 minutes.*

Blend together mayonnaise, cream cheese and sugar. Add egg yolks, lemon rind, juice and vanilla essence. Whisk egg whites, fold into prepared cheese mixture. Pour onto the pastry case. Bake for 45-50 minutes.

Cool and dust with icing sugar.

Felicity and her five brothers (left to right): George Robert, Jeremy, Anthony, Richard and Michael, the author.

* Blind baking means really to pre-bake so that you don't have a soggy bottom. The unbaked crust should be lined with greaseproof paper or foil and then filled with "weights" which can be dried peas, lentils or beans. The "weights" and paper / foil are removed before filling the crust.

Felicity's Sour Cream Chocolate Cake

Never fails!

— Felicity Ryan

SERVES 6-8

INGREDIENTS

6 oz self-rising flour

1½ teaspoons baking powder

6 ounces / 150g soft margarine

4 ounces / 100g sugar

3 large brown eggs

1 tablespoon of cocoa powder

METHOD

Pre heat the oven to 350F / 180C

Place all of the ingredients in a mixing bowl or mixer and beat until smooth.

Divide mixture into two 7½" sandwich tins.

Bake for 30 minutes.

FILLING

5 ounces / 125g plain chocolate

5 ounces / 130g sour cream

Place chocolate in a basin over hot water until dissolved. Leave to cool and then mix in the soured cream. Place mixture between the cake layers.

See also Flicka's Cornish Pasties, page 115

Ruby Anderson Harte (Curry)
Ship at Sea
Etching

Ruby (1913-2000), born in Cork, Ireland, was our biological mother.

Nicki's Chocolate Cake

Back in the mid 1990s, I invited some friends and family for Thanksgiving but I told them I was not going to do the whole "thing" unless I had help. I asked them to come at 10am to help with preparations. In walked a friend with this chocolate cake. Oh, my…chocolate!!! We all proceeded to sit on the kitchen floor and eat dessert first and it was divine. I got the recipe and have changed it to my liking. Now everyone just calls it Nicki's Chocolate Cake. Enjoy and expect to get lots of requests for the recipe when you bring it to our next gathering!

— *Nicki Abbott*

SERVES 20 OR 1

INGREDIENTS

2 cups / 250g organic sugar

1¾ cups / 225g organic spelt flour

1½ teaspoons baking powder

1½ teaspoons baking soda

¾ cup / 96g unsweetened cocoa powder

1 teaspoon salt

2 large brown eggs

1 cup / 250ml buttermilk

½ cup / 125ml vegetable oil

2 teaspoons vanilla

1 cup, just made hot coffee

ICING

⅓ cup / 75g soft butter

⅓ cup / 75g cocoa powder

2 cups / 250g powdered sugar

1½ teaspoons vanilla

1 tablespoon coffee

METHOD

Pre heat the oven to 350F / 180C

Grease and flour a baking pan.

Combine all the dry ingredients in a bowl.

Add the eggs, milk, oil and vanilla. Beat with a hand mixer/blender for 2 minutes.

Gradually add the boiling coffee then the batter will be thin.

Pour into the pan and bake for 30-35 minutes.

FOR THE ICING

Mix and beat with a hand mixer until smooth. Wait until the cake is completely cool before adding the icing. Try not to eat the icing until it is on the cake!

Using organic ingredients really makes a difference. I like using spelt flour because it is better for digestion.

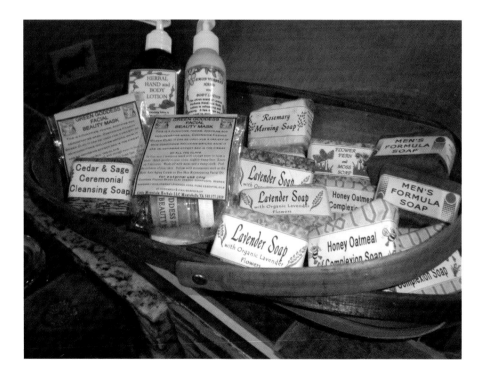

NICKI ABBOTT and her husband Bob live in the mountains of Virginia with the George Washington National Forest in their back yard. They grow a large, spray-free garden where they harvest masses of produce. What is not eaten is preserved and any excess is sold at the Nelson Farmers' Market. Nicki makes a whole line of handcrafted castile soaps, lotions, creams, salves and clinical aromatherapy formulas. Her business is called Little Mountain Herbals and she is excited that she will soon have an ETSY shop.

Grandma McCutcheon's Coconut Crème Pie

My grandmother, Louise McCutcheon, was a legend in our home town of Wausau, Wisconsin. This is one of her "secret" recipes that she refused to divulge, even to family members. She finally passed the secret recipes on to the spouses of each of her sons. She is now long gone and the recipes are too good to be bogarted by any one sibling any longer. This is the Coconut Crème Pie, presented to my Cousin Tom's wife, Rene. It is still the finest pie I have ever put in my mouth. Oh, and be forewarned — the double boiler is not an optional part of the recipe!

— John McCutcheon

SERVES 6

INGREDIENTS

2¼ cups / 750 ml milk

4 egg yolks

¼ cup / 60ml milk

½ cup / 64g sugar

5 tablespoons cornstarch

Pinch of salt

1 tablespoon butter

½ teaspoon vanilla

½ cup / 64g desiccated coconut

See also John's Salsa Verde, page 26

JOHN and I worked together almost every year at the American Theatre. He is a widely recognized true Renaissance Man. An all-around great human being.
www.folkmusic.com

Photo: Irene Young

METHOD

Cook in glass double boiler

2 cups of milk until hot

Beat together until very light egg yolks, milk, sugar, cornstarch and pinch of salt.

Stir into hot milk in double boiler

Stir until thick (NOTE: until mixture does not "run" off wooden spoon)

Let cool then add butter and vanilla

Put into baked pie shell

Put ½ cup of coconut on top

*You can also add bananas or substitute bananas for coconut to make Banana Crème Pie

Maria Paranova's Coffee Flan from Spain

*This was always and is still my favorite dessert. Since I was a kid,
my family would make these at home in Barcelona. Later on, when
I moved on, I added the coffee flavor and the flan turned
out to taste even better! I love cooking and that is something I
miss the most when I am on tour with Les Ballets Trockadero
de Monte Carlo. But when I am home in New York City,
I love to make this flan and share it with friends.*

I hope you all enjoy this unique Spanish recipe. I know I have!

**— Carlos Renedo / aka Maria Paranova /
Boris Nowitsky**

SERVES 8

INGREDIENTS

4 cups / 1 liter whole milk

1 cup / 200g sugar

7 large brown eggs

3 teaspoons vanilla extract

2 teaspoons coffee extract

Espresso shot of coffee

2 tablespoons condensed milk (optional)

FOR THE CARAMEL

¾ cup / 170g sugar

A hint of lemon and a few drops of water

MARIA PARANOVA 's remarkable life story, only now
coming to light after 19 dark years in near hopeless
conviction that she was Mamie Eisenhower, will never
fully be told. The discovery of her true identity (at a
Republican fund raising event in Chicago) brought
her to the attention of the Trockaderos where she is
slowly recovering her technical powers.

METHOD

In a heavy black saucepan, cook and stir sugar over medium-low heat until melted and golden brown, not too dark, adding a hint of lemon and a few drops of water so that the sugar does not burn. About 10-15 minutes.

Quickly pour into little stainless steel flan molds or a 2-quart round baking dish, tilting to coat the bottom.

Set aside.

Preheat oven to 350F / 180C

Pour the milk into a large pot or bowl. Add the sugar and stir well.

Beat the eggs in a separate bowl and add them slowly to the milk. Stir well.

Add vanilla and coffee extract and the espresso shot to the mixture.

If desired add condensed milk for a thicker texture. Mix well.

Pour the mixture over caramelized sugar.

Place the molds or the baking dish in a larger baking pan. Pour water into larger pan to a depth of 1 inch.

Bake for 60 minutes or until center is just set (mixture will jiggle).

Remove molds or dish from the larger pan and let cool. Refrigerate for a few hours or overnight.

To serve, run a knife around edges and invert onto a plate.

Some whipped cream may be added on top.

¡Buen provecho!

Flan is found in recipes as far back as ancient Rome. It was during Roman times that domesticated chickens were first kept for laying eggs. The Romans, consulting the Greek's knowledge of the art of cooking, developed new recipes, one of which turned out to be this custard concoction known as flan. The word "flan", and the earlier forms "flaune" and "flawn", comes from Old French.

BORIS NOWITSKY has been with the greatest ballerinas of our time and he has even danced with some of them. One of the first defective Russian male stars, he left the motherland for purely capitalistic reasons. Amazingly, between appearances on television and on Broadway, in movies, commercials, magazines and special events, and women's nylons, he occasionally still has time to dance.
www.trockadero.org

Betty's Stuffed Date Drop Cookies

This is a family recipe, handed down to me by my mother.
Unusual and delicious! Enjoy.

— Betty Buckley

Oh no…the luggage did not arrive. When I first presented the legendary Betty Buckley in the 1986/87 season, we had to scramble. And scramble we did as she had nothing to wear for the concert. So off we went to Sandy Austin's renowned dress shop in Lafayette and found just the right thing.

— Michael Curry

MAKES APPROXIMATELY 5 DOZEN

INGREDIENTS

1 pound / 450g (approx. 70) pitted dates

½ teaspoon baking soda

1-3 ounce / 75g package pecan or walnut halves

¼ teaspoon salt

4 tablespoons shortening

¼ cup / 60ml sour cream

¾ cup / 100g medium brown sugar

1 large brown egg

1¼ cups / 150g sifted enriched flour

½ teaspoon baking powder

METHOD

Preheat the oven to 400F / 200C

Stuff the dates with the nut halves.

Cream the shortening and sugar until it is light and fluffy. Beat in the egg.

Sift the sugar, flour, baking powder, soda and salt. Add the sour cream and mix with the creamed mixture. Stir in the stuffed dates.

Drop onto a greased cookie sheet — one date per cookie.

Bake for 8-10 minutes. Place on a wire rack to cool.

TOP WITH GOLDEN GLOW FROSTING

½ cup / 100g butter

¾ teaspoon vanilla

3 cups / 380g powdered sugar

3 tablespoons distilled water

Lightly brown the butter then remove from heat. Gradually beat in the powdered sugar and vanilla. Slowly add the water until the mixture is spreading consistency. This frosting yields enough to ice your delicious cookies.

Betty Buckley with Michael Curry, 1986
Photo Philip Gould

BETTY created the role of Grizabella in the smash hit musical *Cats* for which she won a Tony Award. She starred in Brian de Palma's motion picture *Carrie* and went on the headline the immensely popular ABC Television series *Eight is Enough*.

Betty was inducted into The American Theatre Hall of Fame in 2012. She and I worked together in glorious collaborations and adventures in 86/87, 97/98 and in 2006.

Malcolm's Fifteens

I was born and brought up in Northern Ireland. My mother, Lorna McKee, was a wonderful baker and this is her recipe for a traditional Northern Irish tray bake treat. These are called Fifteens because you need fifteen of each of the main ingredients, plus it only takes 15 minutes to make them. They are served absolutely everywhere you go in Northern Ireland from friends' home to cafés.

— *Malcolm McKee*

SERVES 15 IF THEY ARE LUCKY. EVERYONE WILL WANT MORE THAN ONE SLICE.

INGREDIENTS

15 marshmallows (quartered)

15 Digestive Biscuits or Graham Crackers (crushed)

15 glacé or candied cherries (halved)

About 200 ml of condensed milk

Dried coconut

METHOD

Mix together the marshmallows, crushed digestives and cherries in a large bowl. Gradually add the condensed milk until you have a soft, moist dough.

Roll the mixture into a large sausage shape approximately 1½ inches in diameter and then roll this in dried coconut until it's completely coated.

Wrap in cling film and chill in the fridge for two hours to harden. Cut into fifteen slices (of course!) and serve in paper cupcake cases.

Malcolm's Mum, Lorna McKee in the kitchen at Christmas, early 1960's

Highly acclaimed as a writer, director and composer, MALCOLM MCKEE is well known to millions of BBC Radio listeners as the voice of Graham Ryder in *The Archers*. He has composed scores for more than 50 dramas for BBC Radio and has written 16 scripts for BBC Radios 3 and 4 including adaptations of *The Comedy of Errors, Grand Hotel, Oh What a Lovely War* and Coward's *Tonight at 8.30*, among others.

As writer and director Malcolm's credits include the Shakespeare Revue for the Royal Shakespeare Company, in London's West End, Off Broadway in New York and on worldwide tours. The company also has a long association with Swan Hellenic cruises and thirty six voyages have taken them to more than 60 countries from Aruba to Zanzibar.

He has also written and directed productions for the Bristol Old Vic, Birmingham Rep, and Tate Britain and for HRH The Prince of Wales at St. James' Palace and at Highbury where he staged Patricia Routledge and Patrick Stewart in *A Marvellous Party*.

Malcolm is also a Principal Director for the company Private Drama for which he has written and staged more than 60 productions in historic venues including Kensington Palace and Hampton Court Palace and Shakespeare's Globe (among many others).

We first met when I presented the sparkling Shakespeare Revue at The American Theatre and became fast friends. Malcolm brought the company to The American Theatre for five or six shows.

www.shakespearerevuecompany.com

Jude's "Fried Egg Pie"

This is a recipe my grandmother and mother used to make for special occasions. It is so decadent, I rarely make it any more, but it is so much a part of my childhood memories, and I've never met anyone outside my family who has even heard of it. It looks so real, you have to tell people it isn't actually fried eggs just to get them to try it. Then they come back for more!

— Jude Schlotzhauer

SERVES 4-6

Jude with Tapito, *Photo Kim Frost*

INGREDIENTS

3 or 4 fresh peaches, peeled and halved (you can use canned peach halves but fresh are better)

1 unbaked deep dish pie crust

¾ cup / 96g sugar (reduce to 75g if you are using canned peaches)

2 tablespoons flour

Pinch of salt

¾ cup / 175ml cream

Cinnamon to sprinkle on top

METHOD

Pre heat the oven to 450F / 230C

Place the peaches cut side down into the pie crust.

Mix together the sugar, flour and salt.

Distribute sugar mixture over peaches. Pour ¾ cup cream over the peaches. Sprinkle cinnamon on top. Bake on lower oven rack for 10 minutes, then 350F / 180C for 30 minutes. Let the pie completely cool before serving. The "white" around the yellow "yolks" will set up into a sort of custard, and it really looks like a fried egg pie.

See also Jude's Mushrooms with Mussels, page 24

Jude's art work encompasses three categories: architectural commission work, a line of functional pieces such as plates and tiles, and personal sculptural pieces for gallery shows. Installations include some works on public sites, such as a twenty foot mural in the VCU dining center, a sculpture in the Richmond Children's Museum, an outside glass wall at Randolph Community Center, and a hanging installation at the Medical College of Virginia hospital. Most of the work is in private and corporate collections, including Capital One, Dominion, Chesapeake Capital Corporation and three glass walls in a Marine Officer's Club in Iwakuni, Japan.

Letia's Ginger Snaps

*This remains my family's favorite fall and winter cookie.
My mother, Betty Lee McDaniel, made these more
times than she could count, I'm sure.*

— *Letia Drewry*

MAKES ABOUT 2 DOZEN COOKIES

INGREDIENTS

¾ cup / 96g shortening

1 cup / 128g sugar +
more for rolling

¼ cup / 175ml molasses

1 large brown egg

2 cups / 250g flour

¼ teaspoon salt

2 teaspoons baking soda

1 teaspoon ground cinnamon

1 teaspoon ground cloves

1 teaspoon ground ginger

METHOD

Pre heat the oven to
375F / 190C

Cream shortening and
sugar. Add and combine
molasses and egg. Add
sifted dry ingredients. Mix
well. Form dough in small
balls, then roll in sugar.
Place 2 inches apart on a
greased cookie sheet. Bake
for 10 to 15 minutes.

Elizabeth Alexandra Drewry
Don't Cry over a tumble....r
Mixed Media

LETIA lives and works as a professional volunteer, as she laughingly says, and plays in Hampton, Virginia. She has served on numerous Boards and Committees and is currently on the Boards of the Hampton Arts Foundation and the Hampton Education Foundation.

Kacey's Harlequin Pinwheels

These Pinwheels will make you famous.

— Kacey Sydnor Carneal

SERVES 4-6

INGREDIENTS

¾ cup / 175ml very soft margarine

1½ cups / 200g light brown sugar

3 large brown egg yolks

1½ teaspoons vanilla

3 cups / 380g all-purpose flour

¾ teaspoon baking powder

AND FOR THE FILLING

3 tablespoons butter

3 cups / 380g semi-sweet chocolate chips

1-14 ounce can / 375ml sweetened condensed milk

3 teaspoons vanilla

1½ cups / 200g pecans, chopped

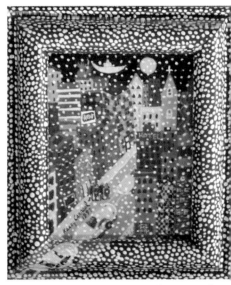

Kacey Sydnor Carneal
Kiki's Team
Oil on Canvas

See also Kacey's Brunswick Stew, page 96 and Shoo Fly Pie, page 238

METHOD

Mix together the margarine, sugar, egg yollks, vanilla, flour and baking powder.

Divide this dough into 3 equal parts and roll with a floured rolling pin between two sheets of waxed (greaseproof) paper, making rectangles.

Melt the butter and chocolate chips over low heat.

Add the condensed milk and vanilla.

Again, divide into 3 equal parts and spread on each of the rectangular dough patties. Sprinkle with the pecans.

Roll up from the longest edge, lifting up with the waxed paper to help.

(Be careful not to wrap the paper into the pinwheels as I did the first time I made these.

Put in the freezer. When frozen, thaw the dough a little and then slice into ¼" pieces.

Bake in a preheated oven at 350F / 180C on cookie sheets lined with foil one rack up from the bottom of the oven for about 15 minutes.

Do not try to remove the cookies from the sheet until they are completely cool.

These pinwheels can be frozen and they will keep beautifully.

Beth's Hazelnut Triangles

This recipe came to me over 40 years ago from a friend
who not only taught me to experiment with baking,
but who was also the best cookie maker ever.
— Elizabeth Reed Smith

MAKES ONE DOZEN COOKIES

INGREDIENTS

4 ounces / 113g butter

8 ounces / 250g all-purpose flour

2 ounces / 50g granulated sugar

1 large brown egg

TOPPING

3 ounces / 75g butter

3 ounces / 75g sugar

¼ teaspoon vanilla

2 ounces / 50g chopped hazelnuts

1 egg yolk

Elizabeth Reed Smith, *Arboreta I, A/P, Drypoint Engraving*

METHOD

Preheat the oven to 350F / 180C.

Mix the flour and butter, add the sugar and egg. Press into a 8" round sandwich pan.

Bake for 30 minutes or until firm to the touch. Do not overcook.

Cream the butter and sugar, add the vanilla, hazelnuts and egg. Pour the creamed mixture over the already cooked base and return to oven.

Bake for 15 minutes. Cut into triangles when still warm and remove from pan.

The hazelnuts benefit from slight roasting. Sometimes I make the topping half as much again just for the added luxury of it all.

Before moving to the United States from her native Great Britain, ELIZABETH REED SMITH exhibited extensively for The English National Trust, The Woodland Trust and many national galleries. She also exhibited in Malaysia, Hong Kong and Japan before taking up residence in the greater Seattle area in Washington. A prolific and highly acclaimed artist, she was an active member of Women Painters of Seattle and mounted numerous solo and joint exhibitions. For many years, her studio was featured in the Arts in the Woods Tour. An accomplished teacher, her work has also been featured in many leading publications and journals. Describing her intricate and amazingly detailed work, Elizabeth herself said: "I seek to blend the precision of the Victorian engraver with a contemporary appreciation of light, color and texture."

Mommee's Mile High Ice Cream Pie

This delicious dessert was a creation of my grandmother,
Myrtle Villarrubia. She used to love making it for holidays,
parties and any and all other celebrations.

— *Daniel Weilbaecher*

SERVES 4-6

INGREDIENTS

1 pint / 500ml vanilla ice cream

1 pint / 500ml chocolate ice cream

8 egg whites at room temperature

½ cup / 64g sugar

½ tablespoon vanilla

¼ tablespoon cream of tartar

1 unbaked pie shell

METHOD

Pre bake the pie shell in a 350F / 180C oven

Once cooked and cooled, place a layer of vanilla and then a layer of chocolate ice cream in the shell. Set in the freezer.

For the meringue — whisk the egg whites and cream of tartar until it forms soft peaks. Add the sugar and vanilla, whisking until stiff.

Cover the ice cream pie with the meringue and place under the broiler for about one minute until it is golden brown.

Freeze again for several hours before serving.

DANIEL WEILBAECHER is Professor of Musical Performance and Music Fundamentals at Tulane University where he also organizes the weekly Music at Midday Series. He also served on the faculties at Louisiana State University and Loyola University. For more than 2 decades, Daniel served as Executive/Artistic Director of the Musical Arts Society — the organization that sponsors the increasingly prestigious New Orleans International Piano Competition. He received his Doctor of Musical Arts Degree from Louisiana State University and while studying in London for two years won the coveted Recital Diploma from the Royal Academy of Music.

Honey Drop Cookies

These always were, and still are, a wonderful treat and were a favorite during my childhood — so many wonderful memories.

— Julie Calzone

MAKES 3 DOZEN COOKIES

INGREDIENTS

1 cup / 8 ounces soft shortening
(or ½ cup / 113g butter or oleo)

1 cup / 220g brown sugar, packed

2 large brown eggs

6 tablespoons honey

1 teaspoon vanilla

3½ cups / 240g sifted flour

2 teaspoons baking soda

Apricot jam

METHOD

Mix thoroughly the shortening, brown sugar and eggs. Stir in the honey and vanilla. Sift together and fold in the flour and baking soda.

Chill in the refrigerator until firm —— or chill overnight.

Form the dough into small balls. Place on an ungreased cookie sheet. Cool slightly.

Put together in pairs with the apricot jam in between each pair.

Bake in a preheated 350F / 180C oven for 10-12 minutes.

See also Zucchini Bake, page 177 and Pfeffernusse, page 229

Elizabeth Reed
Smith
Memories
A/P 1, Pen and Ink

Gloria's Aunt Betty's Kolaches
(pronounced: Ko lah keys)

*These are a common Eastern European cookie, easy to make
but fairly labor intensive. You have to make the dough
and the filling separately. My family is Slovak and Slovenian
and these were a cherished Christmas tradition
that my Aunt Betty passed down to me.*

— Gloria Coker

MAKES 12
THIS IS THE CZECH VERSION

INGREDIENTS

1 pound / 450g butter

1 pound / 450g cream cheese

5 cups / 525g flour

½ cup / 110g

1 beaten egg to glaze

METHOD

Preheat the oven to 375F / 190C

Cream butter and cream cheese then add flour slowly.

Knead briefly into large ball and refrigerate several hours.

Cut dough into 4 pieces, roll out, and fill. See below for filling tips.

Close dough then brush with beaten egg so that it browns nicely.

Place on greased cookie sheet. You will have approximately 12 cookies per pan.

Bake for 25 minutes.

Sprinkle with powdered/icing sugar.

NUT FILLING — 2 cups / 250g walnuts, mashed; add sugar to taste and just enough milk to thicken rather than ooze. Bring to boil, let cool. Should be a paste not runny.

CHEESE FILLING — 1-8 ounce / 200g small curd cottage cheese, 2 large brown eggs, ¾ cup / 96g sugar, 1½ cups / 190g raisins, 2 tablespoons flour. You can also use ricotta cheese. Taste test for sweetness desired.

FILLING TIP — When you roll out the dough to desired thickness (I roll to ⅛ to ⅜ inch) and size, take a butter knife and slice into a grid of squares. I use 2½ to 3 inches squares. Put small amount of the filling into the center and fold over opposing pointed ends. Ideally you can see the filling. Be sure to fasten or crimp the dough with a little water or else it will separate during baking.

Gloria Coker
Photo: Luke Coker

GLORIA COKER was always the one in elementary and high school who was prodded by her classmates to draw the teacher! A good way to get into trouble, as she recalls. Never really intending to pursue a career in art ("too much insecurity", Gloria enjoys a reputation as one of the most well respected artists in Virginia and indeed up and down the East Coast. She received her M.Ed. in Counseling from the College of William and Mary and then immediately joined the staff at the *Daily Press* as news illustrator and courtroom artist where she served for many years.

As you can see from the cover of this book and from her images on pages 6 and 86, Gloria is a superb and deeply sensitive artist. We first met when I asked her to do a workshop/demonstration at The Charles H. Taylor Arts Center not long after we had opened after its renovations. Little did we know that more than 150 people would show up!

Continually creating and exploring new boundaries, Gloria is proud to be a part of the permanent collections of Tom Clancy, JoAnn Falletta, Fuzzy Zoeller, Ernie Els and the Bruce Hornsby family, Michael Curry and many others who choose to remain anonymous.

Working in oils, acrylics and watercolors Gloria conceived an idea of painting important contemporary women. As she laughingly now says, "The idea began and ended when I asked JoAnn Falletta to be a subject because I ended up doing a series of paintings with both the Buffalo Philharmonic and the Virginia Symphony for four years."

With that began her amazing series of musicians, dancers, abstract landscapes that have hidden figures and, most recently, her award winning series of sports figures. But there again, when you check, she probably has a new series going!

www.gloriacokerfineart.com

Leisa's Jelly Slice

I guess you can buy Marie biscuits in the U.S. A round thin dryish sweet biscuit. They are basically the same as the British Rich Tea biscuits/cookies, created by Peak Freans in 1874 and which, of course, found their way to Australia — albeit with a new name! Happy Eatin'!

— Leisa Mather

INGREDIENTS

1 Package / Marie / Rich Tea biscuits (crushed)

6 ounces / 190g melted butter

FOR THE LEMON FILLING

1-12 ounce / 354ml can condensed milk

Juice of two fresh lemons

2 teaspoons gelatin dissolved in

¾ cup / 175ml boiling water

For the Topping

1 package red jello

METHOD

Mix crushed biscuits and butter, press into tray and refrigerate. I usually use an 8" x 12" swiss roll tin. Needs short sides.

FILLING

Blend condensed milk with lemon juice and dissolved gelatin, spread over base and refrigerate until set.

TOPPING

Make up jelly according to the packet being a little light with the water. Cool before pouring over the back of a spoon onto the slice, Chill until set.

LEISA MATHER originally hails from Melbourne, Australia. Having lived in New York for more than 15 years, however, she now calls the Big Apple home.

Her recent theatre credits include Mary Poppins and The Sound of Music at the Westchester Broadway Theatre, Edna in the National Yiddish Theatre's production of Lies My Father Told Me, Camelot, Carousel and Arthur Miller's The Price at the Old Globe Theatre.

She has performed extensively in Chicago and has been featured in national touring productions of *Ragtime*, *The Visit* with Chita Rivera, *Harold and Maude* with Estelle Parsons at the Paper Mill Playhouse and for more than 10 years as a featured performer in the hilarious show, *Forbidden Broadway*.

We first met when she was touring with *Forbidden Broadway* and wowed the audiences at The American Theatre. Leisa was then one of the Five Great Ladies of the American Theatre — the 5th Anniversary Gala in which she performed impeccable "skits" as Marlene Dietrich, Julie Andrews, Barbra Streisand, and probably a few others!

Sharon's Mango Blueberry Pie

*This pie is luscious, juicy, and naturally sweet without adding any
sugar and probably low fat. Once it is made, I will eat it
for breakfast, lunch or dinner.*

—Sharon Isbin

SERVES 4-6

INGREDIENTS

FOR THE CRUST

2½ cups / 300g whole wheat flour

Salt to taste

½ cup / 125ml plus 1 tablespoon canola oil

3-4 tablespoons cold distilled water.

METHOD

Preheat the oven to 425F / 220C

Mix together the flour and the salt with a fork. Stir in oil until coarse crumbs are formed.
Gradually sprinkle in the 3 or 4 tablespoons of water while mixing. With your hands,
form the dough into a ball.

Divide the ball into 2 parts, one section slightly larger than the other. Put the larger
section onto a sheet of wax paper and cover with a second sheet.

Roll with a pre floured rolling pin until the circumference is about 2 inches larger
than the pie plate.

Peel off the top sheet of wax paper and transfer the exposed side to the bottom
of the plate.

Then peel off the second sheet and put the remaining dough to the side.

Prick the bottom a few times with a fork and then bake until slightly golden…
probably around 10 minutes.

Remove from the oven.

FILLING

3 or 4325g very sweet, ripe mangoes

2-3 cups / blueberries

Cinnamon to taste

Peel the mangoes and cut into 2 inch long chunks. Add a touch of cinnamon.

Wash the blueberries in cold water and mix with the mangoes in a large mixing bowl. Sprinkle more cinnamon onto the pie crust.

Pour the mango/blueberry mixture into the pie crust.

Roll the remaining section of dough between two sheets of wax paper and cover the pie.

Pinch top and bottom edges together to seal the pie. Prick the top crust several times with a fork.

Bake 40-50 minutes until golden.

Serve warm or at room temperature.

SHARON ISBIN is universally acknowledged as the reigning diva of the classical guitar. Multiple Grammy Award winner, she regularly performs to sold-out houses in the most prestigious concert halls of the world. She has appeared as soloist with more than 170 of the most renowned orchestras in the world and has created and directed festivals for Carnegie Hall, the 92nd Street Y, The Ordway Theatre and for NPR's acclaimed series *Guitarjam*. Sharon is a regular guest on Garrisson Keiller's *A Prairie Home Companion* and on NPR'S *All Things Considered*. She recently was the subject of a documentary of her life and work, *Sharon Isbin: Troubador*. Produced by Susan Dangel the film was seen by millions on 200 PBS Stations and won the coveted ASCAP Television Broadcast Award.

Her impressive discography now numbers more than 25 titles, reflecting her remarkable versatility — from Baroque, Spanish/Latin and 20th century music to crossover and jazz-fusion.

Sharon studied with the legendary Andres Segovia, Oscar Ghiglia and under the noted keyboardist Rosalyn Tureck with whom she collaborated in publishing and recording landmark recordings of the Bach Lute suites for guitar. She is the author of the *Classical Guitar Answer Book* and is Director of the Guitar departments at both the Juilliard School and the Aspen Music Festival.

Sharon and I first met and formed a lasting friendship when she and Thiago de Mello came to The American Theatre in its inaugural season with their *Journey to the Amazon* concert. Sharon then became a frequent guest at the theatre.
www.sharonisbin.com

Photo: J. Henry Fair

Thea & Peter's North Country Parkin (Gingerbread)

*Tradition has it that Parkin is usually eaten on November 5th,
bonfire night in celebration of the rogue Guy Fawkes' unsuccessful
attempt to blow up the Houses of Parliament in 1605.
But this moist, spicy cake can be eaten anytime — it makes
for a wonderful autumnal dessert. I used to get this
as a kid at my grandmother's house.*

— Thea Musgrave & Peter Mark

SERVES 6-8

INGREDIENTS

8 ounces / 220g soft butter

4 ounces / 110g dark brown sugar

2 ounces / 55g molasses or black treacle

7 ounces / 200g golden syrup or corn syrup. (Tate and Lyle's Golden Syrup is the best)

5 ounces / 120g oatmeal (medium cut)

7 ounces / 200g self-rising flour

1 teaspoon baking powder

4 teaspoons ground ginger

2 teaspoons nutmeg

1 teaspoon mixed spice

2 large brown eggs, beaten

2 tablespoons milk

METHOD

Pre heat the oven to 275F / 140C

Grease a square cake tin (8" x 8").

Melt together the butter, sugar, treacle, golden syrup in a large pan over gentle heat.
Do not allow to boil or burn.

In a large mixing bowl, stir all the dry ingredients together until the mixture
resembles breadcrumbs.

Gradually add the melted ingredients and stir thoroughly.

Add the beaten eggs slowly and then add the milk, stirring well.

Pour the mixture into the cake tin and bake for 1 ½ hours when the cake should be firm and golden brown.

Let it cool and then. Have at it!

If you have the self-control, it is best to store the parkin covered in greaseproof paper in an airtight container for a minimum of 3 days!

The parkin will keep for up to two weeks in the airtight container.

Photo: Christian Steiner

One of the most revered and exciting contemporary composers, THEA MUSGRAVE, CBE, is known for her rich and powerful music which always has a strong sense of drama. She was recently honored by the BBC in a gala of three concerts of her chamber, choral and symphonic works at the Barbican Center in London. Her concerti for clarinet, horn and viola have become standards of the classical repertoire and her large scale works include the operas Mary Queen of Scots, A Christmas Carol, Harriet, the Woman Called Moses and Simon Bolivar which was premièred at the Virginia Opera in Norfolk.

www.theamusgrave.com

PETER MARK served as Founding Artistic Director of the Virginia Opera from 1975-2010 (now Emeritus). His impressive career began as a leading boy soprano at the Metropolitan Opera and then as an acclaimed violinist/violist. Under his guidance and leadership Virginia Opera became and remains one of the most highly respected regional companies in the US. During his tenure, Maestro Mark conducted more than 100 productions in more than 700 performances throughout Virginia. He has guest conducted all over the world and is now serving as teacher and coach to aspiring young opera stars.

www.petermarkopera.com

Bobby's Kahlua Pecan Pie

*This is a custard style pie so it is supposed to just set
and have good color. Be careful, if it is cooked
too long, the filling will be chewy.*

— Bobby Huber

SERVES 6-8

INGREDIENTS

3 large brown eggs & 1 egg yolk,beaten

3 tablespoons brown sugar

1 teaspoon vanilla

½ teaspoon sea salt

1 cup / 250ml syrup

½ cup Kahlua or Cafe Lolita

⅓ cup / 75g melted butter

1 cup / 128g granulated sugar

1 cup / 128g pecans, chopped

1 cup / 128g whole pecans for the top of the pie

1-9" pie shell

Juan Jose Blanco Lozano
Vecinos del Solar
Oil on Canvas
Collection of the author

METHOD

Preheat oven to 350F / 180C

Let the pie shell thaw to room temperature.

Mix the sugars, salt, syrup, butter, vanilla, Kahlua and eggs. Stir well and let sit.

Place the chopped pecans into the unbaked pie shell. Pour the having- sat mixture over the chopped nuts. Cover gently with foil.

Bake for 30 minutes.

Remove the foil and distribute the whole pecans evenly over the pie. Bake for another 20 minutes.

Place nuts into rolled out pie shell and put aside.

In large mixer, using the whip attachments, mix all remaining ingredients except butter.

Mix for 3 minutes on speed 2, then add butter. Mix well. Ladle mixture over pecans.

Bake at 350 degrees for 40 minutes. Allow to cool completely before cutting and serving.

See also Bobby's Meatloaf, page 149

Julie's Pfeffernüsse
Pepper & Nut Cookies

My mother used to make these at Christmas time and for many other special occasions. Try them, you will love them.

— *Julie Calzone*

SERVES 8 -12

INGREDIENTS

1 pound / 450g sugar (white or brown)

4 large brown eggs

1½ cups / 200g walnuts, chopped

1½ cups / 200g currants

3 teaspoons cinnamon

2 teaspoons cloves

½ teaspoon black peppers

1 teaspoon nutmeg

3 teaspoons baking powder

4 cups / 500g sifted flour (to make a stiff dough)

METHOD

Preheat the oven to 350F / 180C

Mix all of the ingredients together and roll into balls about 1" across with your hands.

Bake on a greased sheet for 10-12 minutes.

Inga Charlotte Doerp
The Cat and Mouse
Ceramics
Collection of the author

Sherri's Pineapple Bread Casserole & Italian Ricotta Cheese Cookies

These are two of my Mother's recipes that she made for years. She hand wrote them for me when I left home in New Jersey and moved to Virginia. I cherish seeing her writing on the card. And now I have made the recipes for years!

— *Sherri Fisher Staples*

PINEAPPLE BREAD CASSEROLE
SERVES 6-8

INGREDIENTS

7-8 slices white bread

¾ cup / 96g sugar

4 ounces / 100g butter

4 large brown eggs

1 large can / crushed pineapple with juice (or use fresh — even better)

METHOD

Preheat oven to 350F / 180C

Cut the bread into small pieces. Cream the butter and sugar and add the eggs one at a time. Beat after the addition of each egg. Add the pineapple and bread pieces and mix thoroughly.

Bake in a greased casserole dish for 1 hour.

ITALIAN RICOTTA CHEESE COOKIES
MAKES 4 DOZEN

INGREDIENTS

½ pound / 227g butter at room temperature

2 large brown eggs

1 pound / 450g Ricotta cheese

2 cups / 250g sugar

2 teaspoons vanilla

4 cups / 500g sifted flour

1 teaspoon baking soda

1 teaspoon baking powder

FOR THE ICING

1½ cups / 180g powdered / icing sugar

3 or 4 tablespoons milk

Kacey Sydnor Carneal
Bird House
Acrylics on Wood
Collection of the author
Photo: Gary Pecho

METHOD

Preheat the oven to 350F / 180C

Gradually cream the butter and eggs, beating until smooth. Add the cheese and vanilla and beat for one minute. Add the flour, baking soda and baking powder.

Drop teaspoons of the mixture onto an ungreased baking sheet. Bake for 12-15 minutes.

Mix the icing and beat until smooth. Spread on cookies while they are still warm.

SHERRI STAPLES is a partner at Cinebar Productions in Newport News. The company offers award-winning multimedia services for museums, arts organizations and many other non-profits. They also produce broadcast documentaries and have an extensive background in recording archaeological projects.

Eric's Pistachio Panna Cotta with Blood Orange Caramel

*I am happy to provide one of my favorite desserts
for your wonderful cookbook. This is one that has given me and
my guests a tremendous amount of pleasure, almost
to the point of needing to excuse ourselves...*

— Eric Alatorre

PISTACHIO PANNA COTTA
MAKES 10 SERVINGS

INGREDIENTS

2 cups / 250g raw, unsalted, shelled pistachios

3⅓ cups / 800ml heavy cream, divided

1⅔ cups / 400ml milk

1 cup / 128g sugar

Scrapings from 1 vanilla bean
3 Tablespoons cold water

1 Tablespoon unflavored gelatin

⅓ teaspoon salt

⅛ teaspoon almond extract

A few drops of green food coloring, if desired

Blood Orange Caramel (recipe follows)

METHOD

Preheat oven to 325F / 160C

Spread the pistachios on a baking sheet and toast for about 10 minutes or until deep golden brown.

Set aside 1⅓ cups of the cream.

In a large pot, bring 2 cups cream, milk, sugar and vanilla bean scrapings to a simmer over medium heat. Be careful not to let the mixture boil over. Add pistachios, preferably while still warm. Place a tight lid on the mixture, remove from heat and allow to sit 30 minutes. At the end of that time, return the mixture to a simmer, then strain through a fine mesh strainer or a coffee filter. Discard solids.

Place 3 Tablespoons cold water in a nonreactive 2-quart bowl.

Sprinkle gelatin over the water. Add water if necessary to moisten the gelatin.

Let stand 5 minutes.

Pour hot pistachio cream mixture over softened gelatin and whisk well to combine.

Whisk in remaining 1⅓ cups cream, along with salt, almond extract, and food coloring.

Pour the mixture into 10 (4- to-5-ounce) ramekins.

Cover with plastic wrap and refrigerate for at least 6 hours or up to 3 days.

To serve the panna cottas, unmold them onto serving plates.

To unmold run a knife around the edges of ramekins, then invert onto a plate, and the panna cottas should slide out.

BLOOD ORANGE CARAMEL

INGREDIENTS

12 oranges, preferably a combination of
6 blood oranges and 6 sweet oranges,
  clementines, satsumas or tangerines

2 cups sugar

¾ cup water

½ teaspoon kosher salt

METHOD

Holding fruit over a bowl, peel fruit and separate into segments, removing all white pith and seeds, reserving any juice and set aside.

In a heavy saucepan with a lid, combine sugar and water. Stir to combine. Cook over high heat with the lid on for about 7 minutes. Remove lid and cook until caramel is deep amber. Remove pot from the heat and prepare to add juice to the caramel. (If your fruit isn't very juicy, you may use ¼ cup of water instead of the reserved juice.)

Being careful to stay out of the way of splattering caramel, pour reserved orange juice into the caramel (use the lid as a shield).

When splattering subsides, stir the mixture gently with a wooden spoon.

Return the pot to low heat and stir gently to dissolve caramel.

You may need to add up to ¼ cup of water if the mixture is not dissolved.

When the caramel is totally dissolved, turn off the heat and gently stir in orange segments and salt. Be careful not to break up the orange segments. Refrigerate for up to 1 week in an airtight container.

Serve at room temperature.

Photo: Lisa Kohler

ERIC ALATORRE, Bass, is now enjoying his 26th season with the renowned all male chorus,Chanticleer. He loves performing all over the world and this gives him plenty of time to explore his other passion – food. A part time hedonist and fill time wine enthusiast, he is always looking for another wonderful dining experience. His other passions include promoting Apple products to others, eating his way around the world, being married to his wonderful wife Dorothee and enjoying watching his 2 daughters discover the joys of learning English, German and Spanish.
www.chanticleer.org

Bonnie's Roly-Poly & Whisky Cream

This recipe goes back six generations in my family, originating in Ayrshire ,Scotland and was passed from mothers to daughters through Nova Scotia and down to New England. My grandmother and mother use it for their go-to simple quick desert. When I was touring in Nova Scotia we stopped at the little town of Bass River, which was founded by my ancestors. The first place we walked into was a gas station/deli. I couldn't believe it when I went to pay and there on the counter under a glass case was a pile of Roly-Polies! I thought my grandmother had invented the name, but apparently not as there was a wee sign next to them which read: "Roly-Polies — $1.00 each." I knew I was at home even though I had just arrived!

— Bonnie Rideout

SERVES 6

INGREDIENTS

BASIC DOUGH

2 cups / 250g sifted flour

1 tablespoon baking powder

1 tablespoon sugar

⅓ cup, plus 1 tablespoon (7 tablespoons) shortening

⅔ cup / 160ml milk

FILLING

Soft butter

Brown sugar

Cinnamon

METHOD

Preheat the oven to 350F / 180C

Sift together flour, baking powder and sugar.

Break up shortening into flour with pastry fork until lumps are tiny.

Add milk and stir into dough.

Dust counter surface with flour and roll out dough into a flat thin oblong shape.

Spread soft butter over the entire surface.

Sprinkle ample amount of brown sugar on top.

Sprinkle cinnamon on top of that.

Roll into a log.

Cut the log into slices and place on ungreased cookie sheet.

Bake for 15 or 20 minutes. Be careful not to overcook or they will get hard quickly.

These are like cinnamon rolls only better. The basic dough recipe is also perfect for biscuits or strawberry shortcake.

WHISKY CREAM

INGREDIENTS

10 fl ounces / 280ml double cream

2 tablespoons orange marmalade

1 tablespoon lemon juice

2 tablespoons whisky

1 ounce / 25g granulated sugar

METHOD

Combine whisky, marmalade, lemon juice and sugar.

Add the cream to the mixture and whip until thick.

Spoon into small glasses and chill for at least an hour.

Serve with shortbread, ginger cookies or a roly poly.

Superstar of the Scottish fiddle, BONNIE was another of the most welcome and frequent guests at The American Theatre. Born into a family of Scots, Bonnie holds the distinction of being the first woman to hold the National Scottish Fiddle title and the youngest to have won the US Championship, winning it for an unprecedented three consecutive years. She has been featured on BBC, CBS, and NPR and is consistently played on *The Thistle* and *The Shamrock*.

Bonnie has recorded more than fifteen solo albums and appeared as a guest on dozens of others and she is the author of seven books for Mel Bay Publications.

In 1998, Bonnie and her husband, Jesus, established a nonprofit organization called the Celtino Foundation. Under their expert guidance and care, Celtino has built 19 primary schools in Honduras, Central America. And as for an update on her son Adam, he is now Assistant Director at the Center for Animal Rehabilitation and Education (CARE) for baboons in Africa.

I treasure the gorgeous pewter kilt pin Bonnie gave me at one of her many appearances in Hampton.

www.celtino.org   www.primatecare.org

Linda's Rosemary Shortbread

*Fresh rosemary makes this a very special tasting treat. If,
however, you are creating a cookie plate to give away to others,
wrap or bag these cookies separately as they will make
ALL of your cookies taste of rosemary. Happy Baking!*

— *Linda Christen*

INGREDIENTS

2 sticks / 8 ounces / 227g really good salted butter (softened at room temperature)

1 cup / 120g confectioner's / icing sugar

2 teaspoons pure vanilla extract

¼ cup / about 4 tablespoons finely chopped fresh rosemary

2 cups / 250g all-purpose flour

METHOD

Preheat oven to 325F / 160C

Prepare pan with a light layer of oil. The traditional short bread is baked in two 9" cake pans then cut into pie-shaped pieces. That's too much rich cookie for me so I use a 9" x 12" glass baking dish then cut the shortbread into small squares.

Beat butter, sugar, vanilla and rosemary until well blended.

Slowly add flour until dough comes together. This is not a smooth dough that forms itself into a ball.

Press dough evenly into pan. I use a smooth glass to "roll" it out evenly.
It should be about ¼" thick.

Use a fork to prick many holes in the dough. This is really essential to prevent big bubbles.

Bake for 20 minutes, check for color, and bake for another 10 minutes or until golden brown. All ovens are different, so watch the shortbread closely during that last 10 minutes. It will be a little darker brown on the very edges.

Remove from oven and cool pan on a rack for just a few minutes.

Carefully cut into 1" squares and carefully transfer to a plate or cool pan to cool.

Rick Henson
Linda's Rosemary Plant
Photograph

LINDA CHRISTEN enjoyed a productive and successful career as a "teacher of teachers". Cooking and gardening are her two passions. She writes: "When I was a child, my Mom would never let me cook. Her older sister came to visit often and when Mom wasn't around Aunt Kate taught me how to scramble eggs. I was thrilled and that thrill has never left me. My family and friends enjoy coming to my house as there is always something delicious or experimental (sometimes both) on the stove or in the oven!"

Grandma Eddy's Shoo Fly Pie

*My maternal Grandmother made this pie every
week for us when she came to visit.*

— *Kacey Sydnor Carneal*

SERVES 6-8

INGREDIENTS

1 unbaked 9" pie shell

1½ cups / 190g flour

1 cup / 220g sugar

2 tablespoons butter

½ cup / 125ml boiling water

½ cup / 125ml molasses or black treacle

½ teaspoon baking soda

AND FOR THE TOPPING

1½ tablespoons flour

1½ tablespoons sugar

1 tablespoon soft butter

METHOD

Preheat the oven to 350F / 180C

Mix all of the filling ingredients
together and pour into the
unbaked pie shell.

Crumble the topping mixture
with fingers and then sprinkle
over the pie.

Bake for 35 minutes.

Best eaten when completely cooled.

Kacey Sydnor Carneal
Children In The Mountains
Oil on Canvas

See also Kacey's Brunswick Stew, page 96 and Harlequin Pinwheels, page 216

Wadsworth Family Sweet Potato Pie

*This is stupendous. Maybe you should make it for your
Thanksgiving Dinner as we do every year. Always best to make
it a day in advance and keep on the counter at room temperature.*

— **Susan & Charles Wadsworth, Ahmed & Rebecca Wadsworth Diallo**

SERVES 6

INGREDIENTS

3 or 4 large yams / sweet potatoes

4 ounces / 113g butter

1 cup / 220g sugar

4 large brown eggs

Brown sugar — to taste

Cinnamon to taste but be generous

Good quality Bourbon — to flood the pie

METHOD

Preheat the oven to 350F / 180C

Boil the yams until tender.

Skin and put in a mix-master with the butter, sugar and eggs. Beat until fluffy.

Spread in shallow baking dish. Sprinkle generously with brown sugar, cinnamon and then gently flood with bourbon.

Bake 20-30 minutes. Cover and keep overnight at room temperature.

Right before serving, cover the top with marshmallows, and brown in oven.

Photo: Christian Steiner

Both SUSAN & CHARLES WADSWORTH have been discovering and launching the careers of literally hundreds of today's superstars of classical music for more than four decades. Our friendship goes way back to the '70s when we worked together and presented concerts and residencies for many years.

Susan founded and directs the first nonprofit arts management in the world, Young Concert Artists, and has brought to us many of today's superstars.

Susan has received Honorary Doctorates from several prestigious institutions and she is a Chevalier de l'ordre des arts et des lettres by the Republic of France and was given the coveted Angel Award from the International Society of Performing Arts Administrators.

Pianist CHARLES WADSWORTH originated the world acclaimed chamber music series at the Spoleto Festivals both in Italy and in the US. He established and led the series of concerts at Alice Tully Hall for more than 20 seasons, commissioning new works by Boulez, Bernstein and Barber (among others) and presenting superstars of the classical world such as Kathleen Battle, Yo-Yo Ma, Peter Serkin and Jessye Norman.

Charles is also a Chevalier de L'Ordre des Arts et des Lettres and a Calavaliere Ufficiale (Italy) and the art deco auditorium in Newman, Georgia was renovated and renamed in honor of Charles.

Thiago's Mingau de Tapioca
Tapioca Cream

— Guadencio Thiago de Mello

SERVES 4

INGREDIENTS

1 cup / 128g tapioca

2 cups / 500ml milk

2 teaspoons vanilla

1 Tablespoon butter

1 cinnamon stick, crumbled

A pinch of salt

2 tablespoons sugar

3 cloves

¼ cup / 4 tablespoons oatmeal
(optional — but it does add a good taste)

METHOD

Mix the tapioca, milk, vanilla, butter, sugar, salt and oats in a black pan.

Add the cinnamon.

Cook over medium heat to a high temperature until the mixture reaches a boiling point.

Turn heat to low and simmer for 5-8 minutes.

Serve hot and add some cinnamon powder on top.

Eat with gusto!!

See also Thiago's Avocado Shake, page 31 and Picadinho, page 160

Thiago (right) with Sharon Isbin and the author in the Amazon

Alessio's Tiramisu

— Alessio Bax

SERVES 6

INGREDIENTS

4 large brown eggs, separated

1 pound / 500g mascarpone cheese, at room temperature

2 tablespoons vanilla paste or the seeds from two pods of vanilla. Substitute with vanilla extract if necessary,

A drop or two of cognac or whisky

Powdered / icing sugar to taste. The mix should be as sweet as you want the final Tiramisu to be because the unsweetened espresso will make it more bitter, but the sugar on the cookies will sweeten it a bit.

A few cups, as needed, dark, bitter and strong espresso. Make sure you don't just let the espresso machine run. So keep adding new grounds for each shot.

A pinch of coarse salt

1 package Savoiardi cookies (Italian Lady Fingers)

Bitter (unsweetened) cocoa powder to taste

Dark chocolate (at least 70% cocoa), finely shaved or grated

Photo: Lisa-Marie Mazzucco

METHOD

Whisk the eggs whites with the pinch of salt in a metal bowl until stiff.

In a separate metal bowl mix the cheese, vanilla, egg yolks and sugar until evenly combined. Then fold in the egg whites.

Combine the espresso, having waited for it to cool or having added a couple of ice cubes, and the cognac or whisky. Dip the cookies into the mixture until soft but not soggy.

Layer the tiramisu in a ceramic or glass cake pan of any shape.

Cover and refrigerate overnight.

When ready to serve, sift the cocoa powder and some dark chocolate over the top.

See also Alessio's Bucatini, page 98 and Sea Urchin spaghetti, page 174

Miss Fogarty's Christmas Cake
Courtesy of DANU

One of today's most popular traditional Irish ensembles, Danu's concerts around the world are a glorious mix of ancient Irish and new repertoire. Donal Clancy (far right in the photo) gives the definitive performance of this wonderful Christmas "carol".

As I sat in my window last evening
The letterman brought it to me
A little gilt-edged invitation sayin'
"Gilhooley come over to tea"
I knew that the Fogarties sent it.
So I went just for old friendships sake.
The first thing they gave me to tackle
Was a slice of Miss Fogarty's cake.
Chorus

There were plums and prunes and cherries,
There were citrons and raisins and cinnamon, too
There was nutmeg, cloves and berries
And a crust that was nailed on with glue
There were caraway seeds in abundance
Such that work up a fine stomach ache
That could kill a man twice after eating a slice
Of Miss Fogarty's Christmas cake.
Chorus

Miss Mulligan wanted to try it,
But really it wasn't no use
For we worked in it over an hour
And we couldn't get none of it loose
Till Murphy came in with a hatchet

And Kelly came in with a saw
That cake was enough be the powers above
For to paralyze any man's jaws
Chorus

Miss Fogarty proud as a peacock,
Kept smiling and blinking away
Till she flipped over Flanagans brogans
And she spilt the homebrew in her tea
Aye Gilhooley she says you're not eatin,
Try a little bit more for me sake
And no Miss Fogarty says I,
For I've had quite enough of your cake
Chorus

Maloney was took with the colic,
O'Donald's a pain in his head
Mc'Naughton lay down on the sofa,
And he swore that he wished he was dead
Miss Bailey went into hysterics
And there she did wriggle and shake
And everyone swore they were poisoned
Just from eating Miss Fogarty's cake
Final chorus

Curtain Call

The Spice Market, Istanbul. 2010. *Photo: MPC*

So What To Keep In The Pantry/Larder?

I've always loved the term larder over pantry as the larder evokes memories from my childhood in England. The larder is a semi-chilled room off the kitchen where all the stocks and supplies were kept in addition to the leftover Sunday roasts (under wire "cages") One could sneak in when no one else was around and snag a bite of this week's roast whether it be chicken, beef, pork or lamb. Ideally, the Sunday roast was supposed to last the entire week (or at least until Friday when we traditionally had fish) but it rarely ever did!

The larder was also the place where one stored the "drippings": fat left from cooking bacon or any other kinds of meat. The drippings would be saved for future roasts or fried dishes but they also made rather tasty snacks…we would spread the drippings on bread for a surreptitious midnight treat.

Elizabeth Reed Smith
Buxted Park: Echoes
of Georgian Elegance
Pen & Ink

Nothing Better than Fresh Herbs & Vegetables from the Garden

Grow as much as you can in your own space has been my motto since ever since my first paid job was a a gardener at the 300-acre estate known as Buxted Park. There, in my post high school and college years I learned the joys of cultivating and growing one's own produce and herbs as well as flowers of course.

Annually, I take much delight in growing and harvesting an entire crop of fruits, vegetables and herbs, organically I hasten to add.

Learning to "put up" the produce and to make jams, jellies, pickled vegetables, vinegars and sauces and harvesting and drying herbs straight from the garden is a never ending journey of joy and discovery.

And you will need dozens of Mason / Ball jars with lids and seals to preserve and share all your hard work!

Here Is What I Grow Annually In The Garden, and You Can, Too!

Apples; Blackberries; Cherries; Elderberries (always plant two, so they can cross-polinate); Raspberries and Strawberries. And the following vegetables: Broccoli, Brussel Sprouts, Cabbage, Cucumbers, Eggplant, Garlic, Onions, Peppers, Tomatoes.

And the Following Herbs — some of which do come back every year: Anise Hyssop; Basil and Thai Basil; Cilantro; Curry Plant; Dill Weed; Fennel; Garlic; Lavender; Lemon Balm; Mojo Mint from Cuba; Oregano; Parsley and Italian Parsley; Rosemary; Sage; Thyme

And of course some catnip for the boys, Dhakpa and Nigel.

I also plant or re-seed the following plants to attract bees and butterflies and other beneficial insects: Bee Balm; Echinacea; Milk Weed

Other Herbs & Spices I Always Keep on Hand

Allspice	Cinnamon	Nutmeg
Allum	Cloves	Paprika
Bay Leaves	Cumin	Saffron
Bouquet Garni ...very French	*Fines Herbes* — another great French staple — parsley, chives, tarragon, chervil and lemon balm.	Soy Sauce
Cajun Seasoning — Tony Chachere's / Paul Prudhomme's / Konriko		Tarragon
	Ginger — root & powdered	Turmeric
Capers	*Herbes de Provence* — recipe on page 23	Vanilla Essence
Celery Seed	Marjoram	
Chilli Powder	Mustard — Colman's English, Dijon and Brown	

244

Then The Basics

There is nothing more annoying than when you get deep into a new cooking experiment, you realize that you are missing one, or horror above all horrors, more than one key ingredient. Here is my little guide to having everything one might need in the kitchen:

Baking powder
Baking soda
Barbeque sauce
Beans — red, black, lima
Bread crumbs
Broths — beef and chicken
Bouillon cubes — chicken, beef & vegetable
Canned goods — vegetables, beans, fruits, soups etc.
Cocoa and (milk) chocolate powder
Cooking oil
Cornmeal
Cornstarch
Flour
Gelatin
Ghee (purified butter)
Honey
Ketchup / Tomato sauce
Kitchen bouquet
Lemon juice
Mayonnaise (preferably Hellman's) and Heinz Salad Cream

Nuts — almonds, pecans, walnuts, sunflower seeds, pine nuts, hazelnuts, brazil nuts etc.
Oatmeal — McCann's
Olive oil
Pasta — penne, macaroni, lasagna and spaghetti
Raisins and sultanas
Rice — basmati, brown white and some boxes (6 ounce / 170g) of Zartarain's different flavored rice — they are all good cheer, especially the Caribbean mix and they serve 4.
Shortening
Sugars — raw / brown, granulated, confectioner's / icing sugar
Syrups — golden (Tate and Lyle's), simple syrup and molasses or black treacle
Tabasco sauce or other hot sauces
Vegetable oil
Vinegar — apple cider, herbal vinegars and distilled white vinegar
Wheat germ
Lea and Perrin's Worcestershire sauce

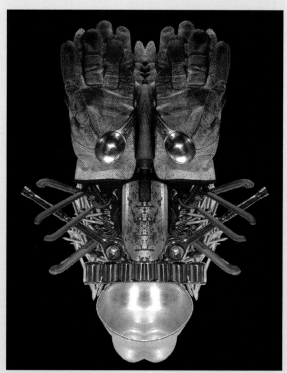

Herman Mhire
Tool Mask
Photograph

Lagniappe*

This is Cajun French for "something added for free, or a bonus."

ORGANIC BUG SPRAY FOR FLOWERS &VEGETABLES

1 Gallon warm water

2 Tablespoons Vegetable Oil

2 Tablespoons Dawn Dish Washing Liquid

2 Tablespoons Baking Soda.

Mix together and put in spray bottle.

ORGANIC FLEA SPRAY FOR CATS & DOGS

8 ounces Apple Cider Vinegar

4 ounces Warm water

½ teaspoon baking soda

½ teaspoon salt.

Mix together and put in spray bottle. Alternatively pour the mixture into the palm of your hand and rub gently into the animal's fur. The spray can sometimes scare them but they love the soothing feel of the mixture and it works!

ORGANIC WEED KILLER

1 gallon white vinegar

2 cups Epsom salts

¼ cup Dawn Dish Washing Liquid.

Mix all together and transfer into spray bottle. Spray directly onto weeds when the sun is hot and there is no threat of rain for a while. Use only Dawn liquid. Sometimes you have to empty out some of the vinegar in order to put in the salts…then replace the vinegar and seal the bottle.

Roxanne Lopez Brown
Tomato
Colored Pencil

Nigel

Dhakpa

Happy cats

Acknowledgements

Copy Editors for Dining Among the Stars, Eileen O'Hagan (left) and Judith Romans.

Writing and assembling a book is a huge task — one that, in this case, has taken more than 2 years and hours of correspondence and research. All great fun, of course. But no undertaking such as this can be achieved alone so, I would therefore, like to take this opportunity of acknowledging the many many friends who have helped along the way to bring this long time dream of mine to fruition.

First and foremost, I would like to thank all of those who so kindly contributed to the book. The generosity of so many friends has been truly overwhelming. And it amazes me that even among more than 150 recipes in the book there were no duplications! It has been a wonderful journey of connecting and re-connecting with friends near and far.

I should also like to thank those who did not contribute to the book but sent lovely notes of encouragement and support. Let's face it some people just don't cook because their life is too busy or they never developed the urge. Such expressions of regret such as" you don't want a recipe from me, I can't even boil an egg" or "you don't want me to send you anything as all I eat is popcorn and oatmeal" still bring big smiles to my face.

Much gratitude is also extended to my great friend and teacher Geshe Lobsang Tenzin Negi for the wonderfully erudite and moving foreword to the book as well as to another teacher, the eminent scholar and Lama, Glenn Mullin whose recipe for Tibetan Noodle Soup and his accompanying essay on the Himalayan way of cooking and way of life are a delightful inspiration full of insight and wisdom. Both Geshe-la and Lama Glenn deeply honored me and the book with their contributions.

My deepest thanks to the amazingly creative Jan Miller and her entire team of designers at Mellen Street Creative. Not only have they made the book look stunning and beautiful, but they tirelessly and patiently worked with me at every stage of the development of the book and its contents. I am so grateful to Mellen Street Creative most especially for this book but also for the more than 25 years of collaboration and working together on *Diversions* magazine, playbills for the theatre, invitations to opening receptions, season brochure announcements and many other ancillary materials they developed to spread the word about our world class programming at both The American Theatre and The Charles H. Taylor Arts Center.

To Gloria Coker, huge thanks for the glorious cover and various other images we have used inside the book. Gorgeous work which set a marvelous tone for the book and for the entire creative process.

And many many thanks to the following without whose participation, support and patience I could never have finished the project:

… my lovely copy editors Judith Romans and Eileen O'Hagan — each of whom spent literally hours poring over proofs and manuscripts, adding their own insights and humor and generally having a wonderful time.

… my brother Richard, for assisting in some much appreciated research — especially on the village and the houses where we grew up in East Sussex.

… my acupuncture therapist, Gary Pecho, not only for being a first rate therapist but also assisting in taking photos for the book and testing out some recipes for me, using his significant talents as a (former) chef.

… my godson Eric Maddux and his fantastic family for their unwavering love and support all the way through the process.

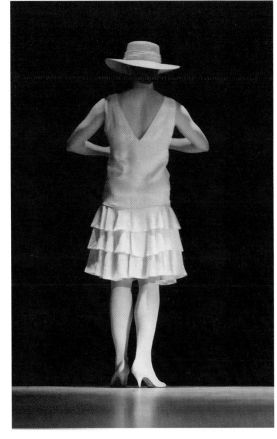

… my entire family — that is all of the Currys and all of the Perrys — our foster family.

… to Ashraf, my companion who has patiently put up with the long hours, late nights, frustrations and joys of creating this book, testing the recipes and simply offering nonstop support.

Finally, to you gentle reader, great big thanks for purchasing, reading and using this collection of recipes. It is my hope that you will find much to enjoy and explore and that you will spend many an hour discovering new dishes and concoctions.

Enjoy.

SUSAN HIGHTOWER in *Beckett Shorts* which I produced for the Virginina Arts Festival. Directed by Christopher Hanna, the production was under the umbrella of my company The Theatre of the Millennium and we also produced Hedda Gabler for the Arts Festival as well as Embracing the Riddle for Actors Theatre of Louisville and for the 50th Edinburgh International Fringe Festival.
Photo and lighting design: Phil Watson

Encore

So, in conclusion, here are some wonderful images of a few of the many magical evenings and experiences of my career as an arts presenter.

MARCEL MARCEAU
Photo credit Roger Pic © 1998

The legendary MARCEL MARCEAU with whom I had the pleasure of working on two separate occasions. Both magic.

MICHAEL and PAT YORK after his great solo show, *Rogues and Vagabonds*.
Photo: E Holt Liskey

JOHN AMOS who brought his solo show, *Haley's Comet* to The American Theatre.

VIVIANA DURANTE As the Fairy of the Golden Vine in *The Sleeping Beauty*.
Photo: Leslie E. Spatt, courtesy of The Royal Ballet.

The fabulous ballerina, Viviana Durante performed with Stephen Beagley in our amazing Ballet Gala in Lafayette. When all of the dancers arrived (there were ten in all) I had just adopted a kitten we found abandoned outside my office. Not yet having named the kitten, I asked Viviana if I could name the kitten after her. She graciously said yes and Viviana became my happy companion and lived to be 19 years old.

Greeting ALEXANDER GODUNOV at the airport before his sold out performance which was filmed as a documentary, *The World to Dance In*.

Escorting the legendary RUDOLF NUREYEV to the after-performance reception.

STEPHEN BEAGLEY and FINOLA HUGHES wowed the audience for the 10th Anniversary of the Fine Arts Foundation of Lafayette.

With the great mezzo soprano, FREDERICA von STADE. I first saw Flicka in the Glyndebourne Opera's production of *The Marriage of Figaro* (with Dame Kiri te Kanawa). Subsequently Flicka and I worked together on several occasions both in Louisiana and Virginia.

With soprano VALERIE MASTERSON (left) and The Earl and Countess of Harewood. Valerie was a lead soprano with the English National Opera, and Lord Harewood was President of the Company. The company came to Houston and New Orleans and we presented Valerie in a solo recital in Lafayette. Lord Harewood was also, during his distinguished career, the Managing Director and President of the Royal Opera House, a governor of the BBC, a widely respected author, and an avid fan of opera and soccer. He also served as the Artistic Director of both the Edinburgh International and the Adelaide Arts Festivals.

With MIKHAIL BARYSHNIKOV (right) after his stellar performance. Also pictured are (left) Bill Como, the founding editor of both *Dance Magazine* and *After Dark Magazine*, and Mrs. Jeanie Rush who hosted the gala reception for Baryshnikov and the dancers from American Ballet Theatre.

With soprano BEVERLY SILLS after her farewell performances with the New Orleans Symphony.

ALL PHOTOS ON THESE 2 PAGES by PHILIP GOULD

PHILIP, a noted and award winning documentary and architectural photographer and author of several books has been based in Lafayette since 1974 (the same year I moved there). He became our "official" photographer and documented the amazing performances we presented. His work has been published in more than a dozen books about Louisiana as well as in many leading periodicals from around the world. www.philipgould.com

Index

Here are Two of My Favorite Photos

Jazz Pianist Justin Kauflin on stage with Candy. *Photo Amanda Reynolds, The Library of Congress*

I am honored to have been instrumental in the launch of the amazing career of rising star Justin Kauflin. It was master drummer/teacher/radio personality Jae Sinnett who introduced me to Justin and we presented him solo and with Trio at The American Theatre three or four times in the very early stages of his now burgeoning career.

And the ever glorious Les Ballets Trockadero de Monte Carlo who usually always sell out wherever they go and keep a smile on your face long after you have left the Theatre Keep on Trockin'!

Michael Paul Curry

Acclaimed as "one of the top 50 Very Important People Shaping Life in Hampton Roads" and voted "Readers' Choice Man of the Year" by *Coastal Virginia/Hampton Roads Magazine*, Michael Paul Curry has enjoyed a distinguished career as an impresario/art presenter and gallery director for more than four decades. He was named "one of the 20 people who have made the most difference in Hampton Roads (Southeastern Virginia's metro area) over the past twenty years" by *Portfolio Weekly Magazine* and "one of the culturally important people " by VEER Magazine. He has been presented to Her Majesty Queen Elizabeth II and HRH The Duke of Edinburgh, His Holiness the XIVth Dalai Lama and President Barack Obama. Having retired as the City of Hampton's Arts Director in 2012 (after 25 years of service), he is enjoying life as a consultant, organic gardener, freelance writer and volunteer in the Emergency Room at Adventist Hinsdale Hospital.

Michael Paul Curry was appointed founding director of The Hampton Arts Commission in Virginia (1988) and The Hampton Arts Foundation (1994). Under his leadership two of Hampton's most historic buildings — The Charles H. Taylor Arts Center (1925) and the American Theatre (1908) were saved, restored and reinvented as vibrant centers and incubators for world class performing and visual arts. Prior to that, Michael founded and directed the Fine Arts Foundation of Lafayette, Louisiana (1974–1988).

Throughout his distinguished career he presented many of the most celebrated artists of our generation. He has the rare distinction of having produced three major Ballet Galas starring the superstars of ballet in the 20th century — **Alexander Godunov**, **Mikhail Baryshnikov** and **Rudolf Nureyev**. As Producing Director, Michael staged productions in Lafayette, Louisiana; at Actors Theatre of Louisville, Kentucky; at the 50th Edinburgh International Fringe Festival in Scotland and at the Virginia International Arts Festival in Norfolk, Virginia. At the American Theatre he selected and presented more than 100 performances per year. He spearheaded two successful major capital campaigns as well as annual campaigns and directed several Galas at the American Theatre which has been acclaimed as a "gem", the "Jewel of Hampton" and "Hampton Roads' favorite performing arts venue."

He began his career as an Assistant Stage Manager at the Chelmsford Civic Theatre in his native England. He was educated at the Royal Masonic Schools where he was Principal Bass in the orchestra, organist for chapel services, and accompanist for choral activities. He also took leading roles and co-directed several of the school's dramatic productions. Following his "gap" year, he undertook a three year course at the University of London, studying English, French and Law. Michael has received dozens of prestigious awards and proclamations. He has served on numerous Boards and committees. He is listed in the première edition of *Who's Who in Entertainment* and in *Who's Who in the South and Southwest* as well as in the *International Dictionary of Biography*. He has had the honor of receiving teachings from His Holiness the Dalai Lama in Atlanta, Mexico City, Washington D.C., and in India both at the sacred site of Sarnath and at Drepung Loseling Monastery in Karnataka State in Southern India.

The Hampton Arts Foundation named the auditorium of The American Theatre in his honor on his 60th birthday in 2012.

Notes